GANDHI AND STALIN

Books by Louis Fischer

•

•

Gandhi and Stalin

Two Signs at the World's Crossroads

LOUIS FISCHER

Harper & Brothers Publishers

New York and London

10-7

B-X

Contents

GANDHI AND STALIN

CHAPTER ONE

WHAT IS THE TROUBLE
WITH THE WORLD?

THE last fifty years have seen inspiring progress. But it has been progress without the assurance of peace and plenty.

The newspapers and magazines of 1919 and 1920 contained numerous prophecies, fully justified, of a Second World War. In the midst of the Second World War, and since its end, there has been much talk of a third struggle. The uncertainty of peace is the major concern of all human beings.

"We have the scientific knowledge to provide an adequate diet for every one of the two billion inhabitants of the globe," said Dr. Charles F. Kettering, Vice-President in charge of research of the General Motors Corporation and President of the American Association for the Advancement of Science. But, he added, three-fourths of the world's population—fifteen hundred million men, women, and children—do not get enough to eat. Man-made, avoidable poverty is the second major concern of all human beings.

The bulk of mankind fears war and suffers want.

Humanity is enveloped in insecurity.

1

Governments and diplomats reflect this insecurity. Each individual reflects it in his urge to forget or in his frantic efforts to achieve security. Political and economic insecurity affects nerves, health, habits, morals, business, elections, and laws.

Some people have enough money to maintain a feeling of economic security. But they know that the peace is unstable. And consciously or subconsciously they sense how wrong it is to be secure when all over the world people are hungry, ragged, and homeless, despite the fact that science and industry could supply them with everything they need.

Baffled by the apparent insolubility of big problems and unable to find the answer to big questions, the insecure seek comfort in self-indulgence or turn to anything apparently stable, infallible, and dynamic which makes many promises. Insecurity brings a desire for political or religious absolutism. Many who are unhappy would give up their freedom for a possible chance of happiness. Despair thus helps totalitarians.

The poor, the insecure, the helpless, the hopeless are the easy prey of dictators.

A secure peace and universal plenty would end dictatorship.

The world is in crisis, and the most distressing aspect of the crisis is the readiness of so many persons to sacrifice liberty and morality in the hope of achieving security. Mussolini made the trains run on time. What did it matter that he suppressed freedom, killed opponents with castor oil, filled the jails, and used poison gas to "civilize" the Ethiopians? Hitler gave state aid to mothers, insurance to children, full employment to workers, vacations with pay to patriots, and symphonies to factory lunch rooms, boasted his own daily, the *Voelkischer Beobachter* of New Year's day, 1939. What did it matter then to Germans and others that he enslaved a nation and prepared to bathe the world in blood?

More steel, more bricks, more guns, more order, more free gifts are the boasts of all dictators. A dictatorship tightens the belts of its citizens and intimidates them with terror, but at the same time it points to the end of the rainbow over the hill where are national might and paradise. Meanwhile, slight advances are paid on the future. To the despot, liberty and principle are nothing compared to a superhighway, a new tractor plant, or another blast furnace.

A wall goes up, a second, a third, a fourth. Soon the builder is in a prison where life is purchased with hard labor and lies.

Statistics of construction are not necessarily the musical score of freedom. Modern Pharoahs have built pyramids with slaves who, having learned the bitterness of bondage, would gladly wander forty years in the wilderness to reach the Jordan of freedom.

Inside the pyramids are mummies: security and secrecy without humaneness; physical strength without ethics. And near the pyramids sits the Sphinx, silent.

Nations may give up butter for guns and become immoral marauders in their quest for security. But where is Nazi Germany today? Nations may achieve partial security by destroying the security of smaller nations and forcing them into their sphere of influence. But later that sphere inevitably clashes with a second sphere leaving only one secure prospect, war.

How can there be individual security when the dictator's secret police can rob you of liberty? What is security under a regime that has no scruples and is therefore incalculable? The mere claim that it builds buildings and provides security has, however, given dictatorship acceptance in many quarters.

The crisis of our era is essentially moral. We live in a world in which the love of freedom, attachment to high ethical values, the capacity for indignation, and respect for human beings have dwindled. This, more than anything else, explains the failure of politicians.

The Sacco and Vanzetti trial and executions stirred America and the world. So did the trial of Tom Mooney. But tens of thousands of judicial murders nowadays never even get into the news. The sins of the Czar's secret police in Siberia, the mistreatment of slaves in the Belgian Congo, anti-Jewish pogroms, and Armenian massacres roused distant nations to feverish passion in the nineteenth century and the first decade of the twentieth. But the millions in concentration camps today rarely evoke even a silent thought. At least one million persons died in the Bengal famine in 1942-3. Five million Jews were killed by Hitler. Millions are starving in China, India, and Europe at this moment. Tito, Franco, Salazar, Perón, and other dictators have extinguished the rights of their subjects. Racial discrimination grows with the intensification of nationalism.

The tragedies and atrocities of our rich, advanced, modern world are so vast and numerous that they elude the sight and emotions of most individuals. Or perhaps we exclude them from our minds in self-protection; it would be impossible to live if these conditions were always alive within us. Some people grow insensitive to cruelty, ruthlessness, and suffering; some cannot bear it. The sensitive person often breaks down and becomes pathological, or takes refuge in ignorance, indifference, and disinterest, or he escapes into his personal life. Outside of it he is too aware of his impotence and insignificance. Hence the widespread disinclination to be active politically or to participate fully in organizations dedicated to the alleviation of suffering and the correction of evil. We contribute a coin or an hour. That is very little compared to the magnitude of the task.

The greater the passivity the worse the problems become and the more scope there is for the blandishments and dynamism of gangster dictators and political charlatans.

Problems succeed problems so fast it is difficult to concentrate on essentials. Conferences follow conferences so rapidly and treaty drafting engages so much mental energy and time that diplomats lose sight of their targets. The road between the First and Second World Wars was paved with "successful" conferences, peace treaties, speeches about the virtues of international friendship, disarmament discussions and promises to be good: Locarno, Thoiry, the Kellogg-Briand pact "to outlaw war" in 1928, Munich in 1938. They kept the chancelleries very busy. After each performance the diplomats preened themselves and crowed with optimism. Meanwhile, a war was in the making.

International and domestic politics are usually seen in terms of conferences, treaties, resolutions, trade, oil conces-

sions, parties, votes, laws, prices, profits, taxes, appoint-
ments, etc. This is not incorrect, but it is incomplete without consideration of the spirit of man and his moral conduct.
Politics requires, first of all, the consistency born of
principle. It has been argued that a social theory produces
consistency. But the history of flip-flopping opportunistic
theorists proves this to be untrue. Adherence to moral principles, however, could create consistency and decency.

Mankind needs an alliance between politics and principle,
and between individual conduct and principle. Often the
two are strangers. Everything is judged by concrete results:
"What does it get me?"

In a dictatorship, politics and principle are enemies. The
end hallows any means; it hallows lies, murders, wars. But
democracy, by its definition and essence, should be scrupulous about means and methods.

Generalissimo Stalin and Mahatma Gandhi exemplify
the antithesis between dictatorship and democracy. It is the
greatest antithesis in the modern world.

In Joseph Stalin, Communist dictator, autocrat of all the
Russias, organizing genius, master of power, politics is ends.
The means do not matter. A pact with Hitler? Concentration camps? The enslavement of small countries? They are
all right because they are means to an end, the means of
getting and keeping power.

In Mahatma Gandhi, saint, statesman, seer, idealistic
Socialist, pacifist, politics and principle are one.

These two men are separated by sharply divergent attitudes toward men, means, and words.

In Gandhi there could be peace.

CHAPTER TWO

POLITICS AND PEANUTS

MOHANDAS K. GANDHI runs a thin weekly magazine, in English, called *Harijan*. He contributes signed articles to it and conducts a question-and-answer column.

In March 1946, a Cabinet Mission consisting of three top members of the British Labor government went to India to reach a settlement about the granting of self-government. They saw Gandhi, Jawaharlal Nehru, and other leaders of the Congress party, as well as Mohammed Ali Jinnah, the Moslem League President, and many others.

Finally, on May 16, the Cabinet Mission published its plan for giving India a national constitution and a national government. The question was: Will Indians accept the British scheme? The real question was: Will Mahatma Gandhi accept it? For Gandhi is the biggest force in India.

Gandhi indulged in "four days of searching examination" and then wrote a page-and-a-quarter article commending the mission and declaring that its plan "is the best document the British government could have produced in the circumstances." The Cabinet members, he declared, "have come to devise the easiest and quickest method of ending British rule."

7

Every newspaper in India reprinted this Gandhi article from *Harijan*. Its text was cabled to Washington for high officials and diplomats to see. Full excerpts appeared in the British press.

Immediately below Gandhi's analysis of England's history-making offer to liberate India, *Harijan* published a second article signed by the Mahatma, entitled, "Mango Seed Kernel," in which he extolled the food value of the kernel as a "fair substitute for cereals and fodder." And he added that it would be good "if every mango seed was saved and the kernel baked and eaten in place of cereals or given to those who need it."

The very next piece in *Harijan* was likewise by Mohandas K. Gandhi and dealt with nature cure, to which he is now devoting much of his time. "Nature cure," Gandhi wrote in the article, "consists of two parts. First, to cure diseases by taking the name of God, or Ramanama and, secondly, to prevent illness by the inculcation of right and hygienic living. . . . Where there is absolute purity, inner and outer," he affirmed, "illness becomes impossible." Then he enlarged on the value of milk: "Buffalo milk is no match for cow's."

This issue of *Harijan* is typical of other issues and characteristic of Gandhi. Because he is interested in the life of the individual—and this life is many-sided—Gandhi is a many-sided man. Time after time in the weekly numbers of *Harijan*, Gandhi turns his attention to the uses to which his fellow citizens can put the "ground nut," as they call the peanut in India, or to answering, for example, a woman who has written in asking him why he does not condemn spitting—to which he replies that he always has condemned it and does so now again.

In one article, Gandhi defines independence for India; in another he urges a reduction in the sugar ration for candy-making; in a third he treats the problem of crime and criminals; in a fourth he expresses the hope that a free India will refrain from maintaining an army; in a fifth he lays down the rule that lying is never justifiable: "Truth-telling admits of no exceptions."

To Gandhi, the mahatma saint, politics is not too big and peanuts are not too small.

One of the most astonishing things about Gandhi is that he lives in public twenty-four hours of every day and seems to thrive on it. His bed is a mattress placed on a board on the stone floor of the terrace of Dr. Mehta's clinic. The terrace is open and level with the earth. Several disciples sleep on the same terrace near the master.

At four in the morning the Mahatma and his group recite prayers. Then he drinks orange or mango juice and answers letters by hand. He is seventy-eight—and says he hopes to live to be one hundred and twenty-five. His hand-writing is clear and firm. He sees well and hears well. Once a day Rajkumari Amrit Kaur, a Christian woman of an Indian prince's family who has renounced everything to serve Gandhi as chief English secretary, reads the news to him from the mimeographed bulletins of a British telegraph agency. He never reads newspapers or listens to the radio.

But India comes to him in thousands of letters and hundreds of visitors. Every walk and talk, and every other act, is timed by the Mahatma's nickel-plated dollar watch which hangs from the waist cord of his handspun cotton loincloth. He is extremely punctual. Interviews usually last an hour and he stops them at the exact minute. He does practically all the talking. He enjoys talking. Indeed he enjoys everything he does, especially talking, walking, eating, and sleeping.

I stayed with Gandhi for a week in a sizzling Indian village in the summer of 1942. I spent six days with him in 1946. I used to walk with him in the morning at five-thirty. The first morning he asked me how I slept. I said I had slept badly; a mosquito had stung me. "How did *you* sleep?" I inquired.

"I always sleep well," he replied.

The next morning he again inquired how I had slept. I said, "Fine, and you?"

"Don't ask," he answered. "I always sleep well."

The third morning I asked him how he had slept. "I told you not to ask," he declared.

"I thought you had forgotten," I teased.

"Ah," he commented, "you think I am deteriorating. How did *you* sleep?"

"Don't ask," I said.

"One or two swallows don't make a summer," Gandhi laughed.

Several mornings it drizzled. "Surely, you are not going to walk in the rain," I protested.

"Oh, yes," he replied, "come along. Don't be an old man."

He does not walk so fast as he did four years ago, but he strides along lustily and is not tired at the end of a

forty-five minutes' stroll. He returns, has a second break-
fast, writes, receives callers, gets a very long massage from
Dr. Mehta, and then sleeps.

Gandhi spends the day—and sleeps during the day—on a
pallet on the stone floor of his room. Food is brought to him
in shining clear china dishes or brightly polished metal
vessels. He subsists on raw and cooked vegetables, fruit,
dates cooked in milk, milk puddings, and paper-thin Indian
pancakes. He does not eat bread, eggs, meat, or fish, and
takes no coffee, tea, or spirits.

Gandhi often stays in a crude hut in the middle of a slum.
The slum is inhabited by Untouchables. Religious Hindus
usually keep aloof from the Untouchables; they believe they
are polluted by contact with Untouchables. Gandhi wants
to wean the caste Hindus from this cruel treatment of
the Untouchables. So whenever possible he lives among
them. As a result, caste Hindus have commenced to use
Untouchables as servants and cooks, and I was told on
every hand in India that the barrier between Untouchable
and caste Hindu is breaking down, especially in the cities.
Gandhi has compelled sacred Hindu temples, closed for
thousands of years to Untouchables, to open their doors
to them.

"I am an Untouchable," he said to me. He is not one by
birth; he is a caste Hindu. But he identifies himself with
the Untouchables so that other Hindus may do likewise.
"I am a Hindu, I am a Moslem, a Christian, a Jew, a
Buddhist," he added.

With few exceptions, Indians bow low before Gandhi
when they come into his presence, and usually touch his

feet. Often he bangs them on the back with his fist and tells them to stop. Then they "squat," as he calls it, on the floor, and the interview begins. Anybody in the house may enter and listen. But normally the talking is confined to Gandhi and the person to whom he has granted an appointment.

Congress party prime ministers of Indian provinces come for his advice and instructions. Educators come to test their ideas on him. Whoever has a new scheme—and who in India hasn't—seeks his blessing. Individuals come to get help in solving personal problems. While I was with him, an Untouchable couple who were unhappy in married life took up his time with their tales of woe. He spent hours with them. Peasants and workingmen request his help in introducing needed economic and social reforms.

I traveled with him by train from Poona to Bombay, on one visit, a three-and-one-half-hours' journey. He and his party, which consists of about ten secretaries and devotees and his doctor, occupied a special car, a third-class car furnished only with hard wooden benches. It rained torrents, and soon water began to drip from the roof. Gandhi wrote an article for *Harijan*. Then he corrected proofs of another article. Then he talked to political leaders who had boarded the train for an interview. At all stations, despite the downpour, crowds assembled on the platform to see him. During one stop, two boys of about fourteen years of age, soaked to their brown skins, stood outside the window yelling, "Gandhiji! Gandhiji!" ("Ji" is a suffix of respect.)

I asked Gandhi, "What are you to them?"

He stuck two fingers up from the side of his bald head and replied, "Horns. I am a man with horns. A spectacle." (He speaks perfect English.)

I marveled at his energy. He never goes to bed before ten; on occasions when I passed him as he lay on the terrace ready for the night he would exchange some bantering remarks with me or tell me that if I prayed more I would sleep better.

Gandhi is supremely religious. The core of his religion is a faith in God, in himself as an instrument of God, and in nonviolence as the way to God in heaven and to peace and happiness on earth. Belief in nonviolence shapes all his political acts, thoughts, and statements.

Several times Gandhi alluded to the two world wars. I asked him why he did not preach nonviolence to the West. "I am a mere Asiatic," he replied with a laugh, "a mere Asiatic. But Jesus was an Asiatic also."

"How can I preach nonviolence to the West," he continued, "when I have not even convinced India? I am a spent bullet." He realizes that the temper of the youth of his country is violent, impatient, and revolutionary.

Gandhi dedicated his life to the independence of his country. Yet he did not wish to achieve that goal through violence. This is now his quarrel with the Socialists. "I was a Socialist before he was born," said Gandhi about Jayaprakash Narayan, the forty-five-year-old leader of the growing Socialist movement of India. Jayaprakash is a startling figure. He studied at the universities of Wisconsin and Ohio, was a house-to-house salesman of toilet articles in Chicago, and has had his share of jail sentences in India. Like Socialists throughout the world, Jayaprakash is very anti-Communist and anti-Soviet. Gandhi loves him and he is devoted to Gandhi. But under Jayaprakash's leadership the Indian Socialists adopted violent measures during the civil disobedience campaign which Gandhi started in 1942. The Socialists practiced sabotage, organized an underground, hid from the police, and forcefully hampered the authorities. All these things are outlawed by Gandhi's code of nonviolence.

Gandhi is therefore at odds with the Socialists although he is the father of their desire for national liberation and shares their ultimate Socialist purpose.

Gandhi was anti-Japanese and anti-Nazi yet he was anti-war because he thought the victorious powers would be incapable of making a peace based on armed might. He looks beyond the immediate target.

The Mahatma sees humanity and even his own India tending toward the pursuit of power for its own sake and the subjugation of the individual by the state and by huge agglomerations of private wealth. Gandhi's economic paradise would consist of self-sufficient villages in farming and cottage industries and a few small towns. He regards himself as the champion of the poor and little man.

Like most Indians, Gandhi is indocentric. India is sick and, it is like having a sick heart; you cannot forget it. Indians think primarily of their own problems. But in talking to Gandhi one sees the entire world in the mirror of India. No discussion with Gandhi about conditions and facts remains on a pedestrian level. He lifts it with a phrase to a higher plane, and soon one sees the topic of conversation in the larger philosophical aspect of the ultimate problems that confront man on this earth.

An American famine mission went to see Gandhi. One member asked whether it was right to feed Japan, an ex-enemy country, while India verged on starvation. "If it is correct," he replied, "that the Japanese are in greater need of food than India then America ought to feed Japan first, for America tried to kill the soul of Japan." He then fiercely denounced the use of the atomic bomb. Gandhi is a nationalist, but his humanity makes him an internationalist as well. His first interest, however, is India.

For Gandhi a conversation with Sir Stafford Cripps and the cultivation of peanuts converge to one goal; the welfare of four hundred million Indians. Gandhi has submerged himself in them. That is why he is the most loved and therefore the most influential man in India. Hindus worship one God, but they also worship many lesser gods and idols, and there are already idols of Gandhi in some Hindu temples.

"The gates of heaven are waiting to receive Gandhi," a hard-boiled Bombay financier said to me. Gandhi wants them to wait; he is working to make the earth more heavenly.

The East is so hungry, ragged, and unhappy, that it thinks with its stomach, sees with its nakedness, and feels with its misery. The hundreds of millions stand in awe of the mighty but they give their heart only to those who renounce personal advantages and dedicate themselves to the general welfare. Gandhi is the symbol of lifelong renunciation and dedication. He lives like Indians and he lives for India. Many differ with him; many reject his quaint ideas about continence, complete pacifism, and nature cure. But all respect his sincerity, wisdom, and passion for truth. When Gandhi contradicts himself, the Westerner says he is being inconsistent; the Easterner says Gandhi is being honest with himself.

Gandhi disclaims wide influence. He says, "I am God's servant." Yet many atheists proclaim themselves his followers because he is the servant of man. Gandhi understands instinctively what Woodrow Wilson once wrote: "Democracy in the widest sense means much more than a form of government . . . it is indeed a system of social organization affecting almost every relation of man to man."

To most people, politics means government. To Gandhi, it means man. The typical politician, as well as the dictator, proclaims himself "a friend of the people." Gandhi, however, is not just interested in people in the mass. He is concerned with people as individuals. He proceeds from the particular to the general.

In 1946, widespread, cruel, and bloody fighting, claiming thousands of victims, took place between Hindus and Moslems in Bengal. Mahatma Gandhi immediately went to the worst area of conflict, a Moslem area, in eastern Bengal. With one or two companions, the frail old man walked from village to village. He begged Moslem peasants to put him up for a night's stay. He received single persons and groups and argued with them in favor of intercommunity friendship. He preached and prayed to all who came to listen. He lived for months among the common folk who had killed and whose kin had been killed. He lived in their huts and ate the same food they did and traveled as they did. He merged with them to understand them and improve them.

An ordinary politician would have made a speech about tolerance and gone home.

When Gandhi's wife died, Indians created a fund in her honor to promote nature cure. Dr. Dinshah Mehta was overjoyed; for years he had struggled with inadequate, obsolete equipment, insufficient money, and shortage of trained assistants. But Gandhi said No. He was not very interested in building up a model institution where a few prosperous persons could go to mend their bodies. He wished to bring nature cure to the peasants and make it accessible to them at their economic level. So he has started experiments, which he himself watches, with homemade and cheap methods; mud packs, sun treatment, diet, water treatment, massage, exercise.

Gandhi is very much the radical revolutionist tugging at the roots of the evils in life. He ambitiously undertakes to lift and change hundreds of millions of people by example and word. By identifying himself in his daily life with the Untouchables, he tries to eliminate the cruelty of Untouchability. When the Hindu-Moslem volcano erupts he pitches his tent on the edge of the lava flow. At all times he lives close to the peasants, for India is a peasant country.

The worker who goes down into the gas-filled belly of the earth to mine coal should live in a palace. But he lives in a hovel while men in palaces fret because his wages rise. Those who fret might try living a miner's life for a month. The haters who would starve the ex-enemy might try living on twelve hundred calories a day.

The gulf between men with power and men without power is one of the central reasons for the evils of the world. The men with power ought to enter into the hour-to-hour life of the average citizen; the average citizen should share, and thereby diminish, the power of the man with power. This applies to governments, political parties, corporations, trade unions, and, in fact, all human institutions. Too much power is unhealthy for those who exercise it and for those who suffer from it.

The dictator has power because he has a monopoly of force. But Gandhi has power without any force. He can neither reward nor punish. He does not hold office. He is a man in a diaper in a hut. Gandhi's influence comes from his interest in man.

Gandhi is an individualist, without force and without money. His individualism does not give him the right to take everything he can get within the law. His individualism is not based on property. It is based on personality. It means that when he feels his cause is just he can stand alone against the world. With Gandhi, individualism is maximum freedom from outward circumstances and maximum development of inner qualities.

Gandhi is a free man from the inside out.

CHAPTER THREE

MAHATMA GANDHI AND
GENERALISSIMO STALIN

GANDHI is the leading champion of India's freedom through nonviolence. When Gandhi's nonviolence is translated into life, however, it becomes much more than negative abstention. It becomes a rather startling and radical philosophy.

Gandhi lived in a village called Uruli, a typical, poor, unhappy village. One night thieves broke into a peasant's hut, beat the peasant, and stole his few possessions. The next morning, the victim was brought before the Mahatma. What to do?

Gandhi said there were three ways of dealing with the matter. One was the "stereotyped, orthodox way" of reporting to the police. Very often, he declared, this merely provided the police with a further opportunity for corruption; it rarely gave relief to the victim. The second way, the one usually adopted by helpless villagers, was to do nothing. "This is reprehensible," Gandhi said. "It is rooted in cowardice, and crimes will flourish as long as cowardice remains."

Gandhi's way of dealing with thieves is "Satyagraha,"

nonviolence. "This requires you," he told the assembled peasants, "to treat even thieves and criminals as your brothers and sisters, and to treat the crime as a disease which has infected its victims who must be cured."

The criminal, Gandhi, advised, must be taught a trade and provided with the means of transforming his life. "You must realize," the Mahatma declared, "that the thief or criminal is not a different being from yourselves; indeed, if you turn the searchlight inward and look closely into your souls you might find that the difference between the thief and yourself is only one of degree." Turn the searchlight inward.

Then Gandhi uttered this broad dictum: "The rich, moneyed man who makes his riches by exploitation or by other questionable means is no less guilty of robbery than the thief who picked a pocket or broke into a house. Only the former takes refuge behind the façade of respectability and escapes the penalty of the law."

"Strictly speaking," Gandhi remarked, "all amassing or hoarding of wealth above and beyond one's legitimate requirements is theft. There would be no occasion for theft, and therefore no thieves, if there were wise regulation of wealth and absolute social justice."

Thus Gandhi's nonviolence leads him to equalitarian socialism. "Today," Gandhi writes in the June 1, 1947, issue of *Harijan*, "there is gross economic inequality. The basis of socialism is economic equality. There can be no rule of God in the present state of iniquitous inequalities in which a few roll in riches and the masses do not get even enough to eat. I accepted the theory of socialism even while I was in South Africa," more than thirty years ago.

Gandhi, however, differs from many of today's Socialists in that he dislikes government. "Don't report to the police," he told the peasants of Uruli. "A reformer cannot afford to be an informer."

"The mind of a man who remains good under compulsion cannot improve, in fact it worsens," Gandhi asserted. "And when compulsion is removed, all the defects well up to the surface with even greater force." In a dictatorship the compulsion is always there. The defects consequently grow worse and finally become dominant.

Gandhi wants to improve the system by improving man. His approach to world problems, and India's problems, is through the enrichment and purification of human personality.

By personal example and persistent preaching, but without a government at his disposal, Gandhi has succeeded in giving Indians a new sense of individual dignity and collective power. Indian women won political freedom, an Indian national language was born. Untouchables saw their status improved, and the whole nation lifted itself out of an age-long lethargy because Gandhi was able to perfect the method of nonviolent yet dynamic and direct action which fuses the impatience of revolutionists with the scruples of idealists.

A friend once asked Gandhi whether on occasions it might not be necessary "to compromise ideals with expediency." "No, never," Gandhi replied. "I do not believe that the end justifies the means." That sets him apart from the dictators and from most politicians.

Gandhi said, "I have striven all my life for the liberation of India. But if I had to get it by violence I would not want it." The Fascist or Communist, on the other hand, will use any means to achieve his end.

The means is, usually, man himself. Hence, the democrat exalts the individual; the dictator sacrifices the individual. The dictator sacrifices the individual in the alleged interest of the individual. Man's welfare is the end, but in the pursuit of that end man disappears into the maw of the impersonal tyrannical state.

Gandhi is opposed to industrialization and bigness. He loves the simple village life. But, as a concession, he writes, "I would have state ownership where a large number of people work together." They will own the product of their labor. The state, however, must not use violence. "I would not dispossess moneyed men by force," Gandhi says, "but would invite their co-operation in the process of conversion to state ownership. There are no pariahs in society, whether they are millionaires or paupers. The two are sores of the same disease."

Gandhi, trusting man's divine spark, would exorcise capitalism and theft by voluntary methods rather than violence. He would use government as little as possible and then, preferably, to support something undertaken by popular initiative. "I think," said Gandhi, "if people help themselves, then politics will take care of themselves."

In this respect, and in most respects, Gandhi is the exact opposite pole from Generalissimo Stalin. Only a few intimates know to whom, or even whether, Stalin is married. The public does not know his house in Moscow or in the country or just where he spends his vacations. When he travels his private train moves secretly; nobody is informed;

nobody is permitted to approach the tracks. At his former wife's funeral in November 1932, Stalin walked through the streets of Moscow behind the coffin. But the secret police had previously cleared those streets and posted special agents in the apartments along the route to keep the people away from the windows.

Gandhi's life is an open book. Stalin lives behind a thick curtain. No dictator comes close to his subjects.

The Mahatma hopes to cure the thief. The Kremlin, in April 1935, introduced the death sentence for child criminals twelve years of age or older. Gandhi did not want his peasants to inform on the burglar. The Bolshevik regime expects sons and daughters to inform on their parents.

Gandhi is incapable of malice or hate. A dictatorship is based on hate and relentless persecution. In the early, less rigorous days of the Bolshevik dictatorship, Lenin advised the Menshevik leader, Martov, and several other political opponents to get out of Russia in order to avoid arrest. But now the gates of the Soviet Union are shut tight. No anti-Soviet refugees have been allowed to leave Russia since 1922.

Stalin was born in Georgia among the wild, rugged, excitingly beautiful mountains of the Caucasus. Until very recently, Georgians engaged in blood feuds, and a fight was not ended except by death.

Long before any differences had arisen between them on economic policies or the question of world revolution, Stalin had quarreled with Trotsky. They were rivals during the civil war from 1918 to 1921. Trotsky's name was coupled with Lenin's as the makers of the revolution; it was always "Lenin and Trotsky." Trotsky was the mighty orator, the master of exquisite prose. He possessed a broad education; knew philosophy and history. He spoke fluent French, German, and English. He knew the world and the world knew him. Stalin, on the other hand, had played an important part in the launching of the revolution in 1917, but far less important than Trotsky's, and much less conspicuous. Stalin is no orator, no writer. He speaks no foreign language.

I have sat through a six-and-a-quarter-hour interview with Stalin. He is solid, strong-willed, capable, and there is great power in his steadiness, complete self-control and utter calm. But he lacks Trotsky's magnetism and flamboyance. He does not win through charm or brilliance. He forged to the peak by consolidating his party support, by intrigues and manipulations, and by his organizing ability. He rose to the top over the bodies of his colleagues, notably Leon Trotsky, whom he hated with a hot hate.

Stalin had started undermining Trotsky's position during Lenin's lifetime, so that when Lenin died in 1924, his natural successor, Trotsky, was barred from supreme power. Indeed, Stalin and his friends suppressed Lenin's last political testament which proposed "to the comrades to find a way to remove Stalin." A triumvirate consisting of Stalin, Zinoviev, and Kamenev took over after Lenin. With the help of Zinoviev and Kamenev, Stalin continued the destruction of Trotsky's reputation. No means were too reprehensible. Books were published in Soviet Russia about the Red Army in which Trotsky, its organizer and first commissar, was not mentioned once.

Finally, Trotsky was eliminated from the leadership.

He went into open opposition. In 1929, he was arrested and exiled to far-off Turkestan.

Thousands of miles from Moscow, surrounded by GPU agents, Trotsky nevertheless bothered Stalin. Trotsky still had tremendous prestige with the army, with the youth whom he had inspired in battle, and with the people. That was before the day of the execution of Soviet leaders. So Trotsky was banished to Turkey. That did not pacify Stalin. He put pressure on Turkey to expel Trotsky. Trotsky went to France. Stalin put pressure on the French government, and before long Trotsky had to move to Norway. In Norway, Trotsky's life was made miserable by local Communists and other Soviet stooges. Trotsky left for Mexico. There he was murdered.

Having demolished Trotsky with the help of Zinoviev and Kamenev, Stalin formed an alliance with Bukharin, Rykov, and Tomsky to oust Zinoviev and Kamenev. Once Stalin and Kamenev were photographed with Lenin, Stalin on one side, Kamenev on the other. Stalin cut out Kamenev, and the picture of himself with Lenin was then circulated in millions of copies. Zinoviev and Kamenev had been Stalin's closest co-workers, and Lenin's closest co-workers. But Stalin pursued a policy of political character assassination until, at last, things came to a point where Zinoviev and Kamenev were executed.

Later Bukharin and Rykov, who had helped Stalin against Zinoviev and Kamenev, were executed after one of the famous Moscow trials. Tomsky, the head of the Soviet trade-union movement, committed suicide before he could be arrested.

Stalin stood on the pinnacle; below were his puppets.

Now a systematic campaign was commenced to persuade the public of Stalin's qualities. On every possible occasion, on millions of occasions, Stalin's name and Stalin's photograph were coupled with Lenin's. Stalin had taken the place of Trotsky.

Since then, Stalin has shaped the Soviet system. Its decrees, policies, literature, and institutions bear his clear imprint.

Gandhi is judged by his words and acts, by his life.

Stalin is judged by these and by Russia. He has re-created Russia in his image.

Under Stalin's leadership, the Soviet Union has accomplished great deeds. Many new cities and many new gigantic, modern plants have been built. Russia has become a big industrial power. She is not independent economically. No country is. But with the new factories constructed and the new natural resources discovered by indefatigable Soviet scientists, she can stand on her own feet much better than ever. During the Second World War, American Lend-Lease helped Russia win, but without the output of the industries established at home in accordance with Stalin's policies and without his lavish expenditure of manpower, Germany might have conquered the Soviet Union.

As a result of victory, and thanks to Stalin's vigorous diplomacy, Russia has annexed vast foreign territories. Stalin has made Russia bigger and stronger. He is thus in the tradition of Ivan the Terrible, Peter the Great, and Catherine the Great, who contributed to Russia's imperial expansion and who accordingly receive high praise in Soviet literature.

More historic even than these epochal developments is Stalin's collectivization of Soviet farming. Virtually all Soviet agricultural land is owned by the state and cultivated in one of two ways: as government farms where the employees get wages on a piecework basis and the crops go to the government, or as collective farms. There are hundreds of thousands of collectives in the Soviet Union. Almost all Soviet agriculture is carried out by the collectives. A collective is a village which uses government-owned land and government-owned machinery and gives a large share of its harvest to the government. The rest is divided among the peasants in proportion to their work on the collective's land. In addition, each peasant has a little patch of land for his own use, rarely more than an acre, on which he can raise vegetables, chickens, pigs, etc. These are for family consumption; surpluses, if any, may be sold on the market. No collectivized peasant—and more than 95 per cent of the Soviet farm population is collectivized—is permitted to own a horse, ox, plow, truck, or tractor. Those are capital, and the state is the only capitalist.

Collectivization is the first change that has taken place in the organization of agriculture since the serfs of Europe were liberated. It is a more scientific way' of tilling the earth. In theory, it combines large-scale cultivation with individual initiative. That was the original idea behind collectivization. But the Soviet system as molded by Stalin has perverted the idea. The collectivized peasant is, in fact, a serf completely under the thumb of the government which supplies his land, tools, and seed, and which markets the bulk of his yield.

The collective farm looks like advanced socialism but actually it is a state institution, and there is no freedom in it. The form is the form of socialism but the spirit is the spirit of Stalin: regimentation and domination from above and outside. In each collective, a few Communists carry out the will of the Kremlin.

The Soviet collectives illustrate the major weakness of Stalin's technique. There are no landlords. There are no grasping merchants. Normally, this ought to make the peasants work hard; they are working for themselves and for a government which is their government. But that is not what happens. The Kremlin has had to introduce the most complete system of piecework pay. Peasants in collectives, like factory hands, are paid in accordance with the amount and nature of their labor. Should that not stimulate enough effort? It does not. The Soviet authorities in Moscow are found organizing a tremendous, nation-wide campaign whenever it is time to plow, to plant the spring crop, to plant the winter crop, to harvest. Why should peasants be urged to plow and plant? It is the natural instinct of the farmer to till the soil and gather in its fruits. But all the big urban newspapers, in Moscow, in Leningrad, in the many densely populated industrial cities of Russia, print long, front-page editorials year in and year out screaming and scolding about delayed plowing, about the lag in planting, about crops rotting on the fields, about tractors unrepaired. What has the city to do with those things? Why tell townspeople what peasants ought to be doing?

The *Literary Gazette* is the weekly magazine, published in Moscow, of the "Directorate of the Union of Soviet

Authors of the Soviet Union." (Note, incidentally, that it is not the magazine of the Authors' Union. It is the magazine of the "Directorate.") In its issue of March 1, 1947, the publication devotes its full four pages, newspaper size, to one item. The item covers all of page one, all of page two, all of page three, and all of page four. There is nothing else in the paper but this single item. The item is the text of a resolution passed by the Central Committee of the Soviet Communist party; only the verbatim text; no comment. The resolution is entitled, "Regarding the Measures for the Improvement of Agriculture in the Post-War Period."

The order had gone out that every publication in the Soviet Union was to print this resolution, and so the *Literary Gazette* gave over an entire issue to it. The authors had read it in their daily newspapers. But the *Literary Gazette* did not dare to omit it or even to summarize it. Nobody dares modify instructions from the top of the pyramid.

The resolution for the improvement of agriculture is a ukase to the local authorities to increase the acreage under cotton, sugar beets, flax, grass, etc., to increase the size of herds, to improve irrigation, to improve the work of tractor squads, etc. Then it affirms that "in recent years" many things have gone wrong on the collective farms. Concretely, it complains of "the stealing of the nationalized lands of the collectives and the removal of the wealth of the collectives—equipment, cattle, other property and money . . ."

The local authorities are instructed to cure these ills. But perhaps they are rooted in the undemocratic domination of the collectives by Communist party members and in the violent origins of the collectives back in 1929 to 1933, when millions of peasants were forced into the collectives whether they wished to join or not. To vent their wrath, the peasants slaughtered millions of heads of cattle before entering the collectives. They refused to surrender their personally owned cattle to the collectives. Today, the collectivized peasants steal the property and wealth of the collectives. Why? Obviously, because though the peasants have been coerced into the collectives, they continue to distinguish between "theirs," the government's, and "mine." The peasants are in the collectives, but the spirit of collectivism is lacking. In the Jewish collectives in Palestine, which are real because they are voluntary, stealing of communal property or money is unheard of and inconceivable, and there is naturally no piecework. Everybody works as hard as he can and shares alike in the products of the labor.

A dictatorship can handle big tasks—Stalin herded a hundred million peasants into the collective farms. But it cannot handle delicate tasks. It has not been able to remake the psychology of the peasants. Its methods are wrong.

Stalin keeps authority and initiative at the peak of the pyramid. A dictatorship must do that because it is a dictatorship. As a result, nothing works automatically in Soviet Russia. Everything is a "campaign." The planting of wheat is a campaign, and the cutting of timber is a campaign, and terrific energy is generated at "the center" —Moscow—to start and conduct these campaigns.

The nature of a regime is not determined solely by its attitude toward the nationalization of factories or of land. For it could favor these and be Fascist. What is decisive is the relationship of a regime to political parties and trade-unions and local authorities. If a government believes that political parties, trade-unions, and city and village self-rule are no longer necessary now that it is in power, then it is an autocracy no matter what it has done about the nationalization of factories and farms.

The character of a government is determined not by its treatment of inanimate property but by its treatment of living people. A social system might free land from private ownership and put serfs on the free land. It might liberate factories from capitalist possession and enslave workers in those factories.

Land reforms, nationalization, and planning must be studied for their effects on human beings.

The saddest failure of Stalin's Russia is the gradual and now almost total disappearance of popular participation in the mechanics, let alone the actuality, of political control. Like the collectives, the co-operative stores have been state-ified; they are state stores. Similarly, collective bargaining by Soviet trade unions ended in 1935. Since then the manager of a factory and the director of an office hires, fires, and fixes wages unilaterally.

All this is the negation of economic democracy. It is economic autocracy.

The soviets, or village and city governing councils, were for a short time the vehicle of common-man, town-meeting government. They are now bureaucratic administrations run by paid Communist officials; the people's voice is not heard.

This is the negation of political democracy. It is political autocracy with Stalin as autocrat.

Stalin is likewise responsible for the rapid and extensive spread of Soviet education from kindergarten to university and special higher institutes. In my fourteen years as a foreign correspondent in the Soviet Union, during which time I learned to speak Russian fluently, I traveled to many corners of the country. Everywhere I encountered a positive appreciation of the new possibilities to study and advance. Poor workers, peasants, and mountaineers felt that under the Czar they would still be illiterate, but now, as many a mujhik mother boasted, "One of my sons is a teacher, another is an officer in the Red Army, and my daughter is a foreman in a factory. I myself can read the newspaper."

The purpose of Soviet education is to promote technical proficiency, service to the state, and unquestioning approval of leadership. Millions have learned to read and write. But they cannot read or write what Stalin does not like. Foreign newspapers and magazines are barred from circulation. Soviet newspapers and magazines, and the Soviet radio are closely screened by fearful censors. Only those foreign books are translated which praise the Soviet Union or criticize some phase of life in a democratic nation. Soviet authors toe the line; otherwise they don't get published. Or they disappear in the never ending purge. Favorable reference to, and any writings by, Trotsky, Bukharin, Radek, and the other Soviet giants who were purged, are meticulously deleted from Soviet encyclopedias, history books, and textbooks. A few special libraries keep the books of Stalin's opponents but do not hand them out except by the permission of the topmost officials.

(Some people call this democracy.)

Stalin is very much interested in Soviet literature,

theater, music, sculpture, architecture, and painting. He makes sure that writers and artists are extremely well paid; indeed, they are probably the richest people in the Soviet Union. Stalin has often intervened personally to get some of them good apartments or vacations at resorts.

One evening, Stalin went to see *Lady Macbeth of Mtsensk*, an opera by Shostakovitch, the best-known Soviet composer. The opera mocked the vulgar middle class of czarist times. It had received, up till this time, glowing reviews in the big newspapers like *Pravda* and *Izvestia*, as well as in the lesser dailies and weeklies, and theater periodicals. The Soviet authorities had helped to have it staged abroad where it won favorable comment. When the International Theater Festival visited Moscow, the Soviet tourist bureau immediately drew the attention of the foreigners to *Lady Macbeth of Mtsensk*. It had been running in Moscow and in other cities to packed houses for several years. Stalin did not like it. The next day he summoned David Zaslavsky of *Pravda* and condemned Shostakovitch's opera as unmelodious and horrible. Zaslavsky recorded Stalin's view in an article. Other papers straightway echoed *Pravda* though they had previously praised *Lady Macbeth* to the skies. The opera was banned throughout the Soviet Union. Shostakovitch was attacked as a bad musician. Nothing he had written was performed again until many months later when Stalin gave the signal to lift the ban.

A few evenings after he saw *Lady Macbeth*, Stalin attended an opera by a young Soviet composer named Dzerzhinsky. He liked the melody. Dzerzhinsky became the object of fulsome acclaim.

Stalin's likes are law. He is no musician. He had no

training as a musical critic. But he is the dictator and he has no humility. Hitler behaved the same way about painting.

The dictator is all-wise. He must be the best military strategist, the keenest economist, the first expert on art, the greatest patriot of his country. He must have a finger in everything.

Boris Pilnyak was a prominent Soviet novelist. His novel *The Volga Flows into the Caspian Sea* had a big sale in Soviet Russia. So did most of his books. Once he applied for a Soviet passport to travel in foreign countries. The application was rejected. Several of his works had been published abroad so he had foreign currency to spend. Lack of money, therefore, could not have been the reason his plea was turned down. He applied again and received a second refusal. Then he wrote a short note to Stalin. That day a courier brought a personal letter from Stalin promising to intervene with the proper authorities on Pilnyak's behalf. In a few days Pilnyak had his passport and took his trip abroad.

Several American correspondents asked to visit the Urals and Siberia. Foreign Minister Molotov refused. Stalin overruled Molotov and granted the permission.

This is part of the technique of dictatorship. The "Boss" must be all-powerful and benevolent—just as they used to say in Nazi Germany that Hitler did not know the terrible things that were happening; "he would never tolerate them." The system strives to portray the dictator as better than anyone else. Nobody would dare to be better than the dictator.

The Soviet government has given special care to children. Its means are limited, for the country is poor, but it gives the young generation the best there is. The Pioneers, the Soviet equivalent of Boy and Girl Scouts, use a slogan which appears in banners, placards, etc. It reads: "Thank you, Comrade Stalin, for a happy life."

Every gesture of Stalin's, every word and smile is carefully calculated for political effect. Stalin was present when Nazi Foreign Minister Von Ribbentrop and Soviet Foreign Minister Molotov signed the Russian-German pact in Moscow in August 1939. Stalin had never before attended the ceremonial signing of a treaty. He was photographed wearing a smile. That served notice to Russia and the world that he was pleased and that the pact had his personal approval.

One day in October 1935, the Moscow *Pravda* announced sensationally that "Comrade J. Stalin arrived in Tiflis to visit his mother. After spending the entire day with her, Comrade Stalin left . . . for Moscow." Then Stalin's mother, who had never been mentioned in the Soviet press before, was repeatedly interviewed. The news of Stalin's visit was hailed in editorials and articles. Communists who did not care for their aged parents were condemned at meetings. *Pravda* of December 11, 1935, published a story of the mistreatment of an old mother.

Such personal publicity for Soviet leaders is extremely rare. But Stalin had apparently decided that the relations of grownups to their parents needed correction. At about the same time, Soviet citizens were instructed to be polite in streetcars. Communist husbands were lectured on the shame of neglecting the children they had with divorced wives. Immediately, party members in Moscow telephoned women whom they had left years ago and had not seen for years and inquired whether they might come to have a look at "little Lenochka" or "little Vaska." It was a great change, on compulsion.

Modern autocracies penetrate into parlor, bedroom, and artist's studio as well as into factory, office, and farm. A recent Soviet decree prohibits Soviet citizens from marrying foreigners. All dictatorships undertake to increase the number of children per family. The Russian government grants prizes and national honors to mothers of ten or more children. Stalin is the father of this policy. When I interviewed Soviet Health Commissar Kaminski in 1936 and discussed the antiabortion law which outlawed abortions while birth-control information and paraphernalia and hospital beds, housing, diapers, etc. were scarce, he said, "The boss wants more children."

The word of "the Boss" ends every argument in Soviet Russia. "The Boss" is always right. But Gandhi says, "I am never sure I am right." Because he is not sure he is right, Gandhi is ready to listen and change his mind. The dictator must be rigid, harsh, unyielding.

Gandhi often blames himself. Stalin blames others. Gandhi is generous to opponents and tries to convert them. Stalin suppresses them.

Stalin gets obedience.

Gandhi gets love and loyalty.

CHAPTER FOUR

IS THERE FREEDOM IN RUSSIA?

THE quality of a democracy depends on the loyalties of persons to persons without the intervention of the government. In a dictatorship, however, personal relations represent a maximum of politics and a minimum of morality. The citizen of a dictatorship develops powerful neck muscles looking around at the authorities. Practically all personal relations in a dictatorship are directly influenced by the state.

The Soviet purges have taken a terrible toll of life and liberty. But their most devastating effect has been the extinction of friendship. Friendship is based on unrestrained confidence and on perfect frankness and honesty. Friendship is fed by communication, by conversation. There is much talk in Russia, but there is little conversation.

The primary loyalty in Russia is to the state. If a friend tells you something that reveals his doubts about the regime or his opposition to the leadership, it is your duty to report him. If it is discovered that you knew and did not report, you will get into trouble. If your friend is arrested—and since almost everybody works for the zealous government anybody may be arrested—you must volunteer to tell all you know. Confidence and frankness die in such circum-

37

stances. You do not share your innermost thoughts with your friend, or your wife, or your eldest son.

Communists, like Fascists, abuse the best in men. And they abuse words by bending them to their ends. Gandhi was asked at a public meeting to comment on Communists. "It seems," he replied, "they do not make any distinction between fair and foul, between truth and falsehood. They deny the charge," he said in fairness to them, "but their reported acts seem to sustain it."

Abuse of men is human slavery. Abuse of words is intellectual slavery. Both are a denial of freedom. When a democracy limits the freedom of men, minds, and words, it becomes similar to a dictatorship and thereby loses some of its capacity to defend itself against dictatorship.

The more gandhiesque a democracy the less stalinist and hitlerite it is.

Democracies should therefore inscribe on tablets of stone a list of the characteristics of dictatorship and add: "Thou shalt not succumb to these."

1. Official glorification of the infallible leader ("Heil Hitler," "The Great Stalin," "Duce, Duce, Duce," "Franco, Franco, Franco," "Tito, Tito, Tito").

2. Intolerance of political opposition.

3. Frequent use of force to punish and terrorize.

4. Discouragement of independent thinking or doing; uniformity.

5. Disloyalty to persons.

6. Insistence on abject loyalty to the state.

7. Absolutism of thought (one's own system can never be wrong, the other fellow's is never right).

8. Indifference to the regime's cost in lives, happiness, and morals; unscrupulousness in the pursuit of a goal.

9. Cynicism.

10. Distortion of history.

11. Incessant propaganda at home and abroad about the virtues of the system.

12. Unbridled attacks on outsiders and unbelievers.

13. Irritation over foreign criticism.

14. Cruel, official criticism of the little fellow but no criticism of the government, the dictator or his favorites in the palace guard unless they have been marked for a purge.

15. Secrecy.

16. Inaccessibility of leaders to the public.

17. Encouragement of big families.

18. Large armed forces.

19. Desire for conquest and expansion.

20. Fear of appearing weak.

21. Exaggeration of foreign hostility to strengthen domestic patriotism.

22. Resistance to changes in the political system.

23. Frequent shifting of officials.

24. Increasing limitation of individual liberty.

25. Subjugation of trade unions to the state.

26. Political impotence of everybody except the dictator and the secret police; personal insecurity.

27. Subordination of the judiciary and legislature to the executive.

28. Disregard of constitutions and laws.

29. Use of "circuses," parades, ceremonies, expeditions, etc., to divert the masses.

30. Complete dependence of the individual on the state.

31. Readiness of the individual to curry favor with the state even at the expense of conscience.

32. Ultimate atrophy of conscience.

All these characteristics of dictatorship add up to the aggrandizement of government and the helplessness of persons—Gandhi's teachings in reverse.

Democracy's chief purpose, on the other hand, is the development of the individual with the aid of the state, but with curbs on the state lest it crush or squeeze the individual.

Democracy should protect the electoral majority against a forceful minority. It should also protect minorities against the majority, and minorities from one another.

Democracy is the right to speak, worship, assemble, and vote. Democracy also should be the right to a job, to free education, to social security, and to old-age pensions.

Democracy means inalienable rights under law. In Russia, individuals enjoy certain benefits and privileges, but they are the gift of the state and can, therefore, be withdrawn. This means that under the Soviets there are no rights; a right is only a right when it cannot be taken away. Nor is there law. The omnipotent state, having liquidated all rival sources of power, is above law—a law unto itself. A law is a law when it applies to the government as well as to the average citizen. A dictatorship, accordingly, is a lawless regime in which the individual is helpless against the state.

The cave man with a club had power over one person or ten persons. The dictator can dominate a hundred million persons through his control of the press, radio, school system, secret police, government apparatus, and jobs. The medieval artisan hired two apprentices. The automobile manufacturer hires hundreds of thousands of workers. One capitalist may have more influence over more men than an entire government in the Middle Ages.

With the advance of civilization the average individual needs more protection. He is helpless without the state and large economic enterprises. Yet, at the same time, he can also be reduced to helplessness by them. This is the great unsolved dilemma of the modern age.

Dictatorships demonstrate the evil in highly concentrated government authority. Democracy is the right to criticize and remove the government or any of its members. No European or Asiatic dictator has ever been voted out of office. Under the one-party or totalitarian system he could not be. In a democracy, the periodic supplanting of one party by the other, even if the contending parties are not very dissimilar in principle and platform, is healthy. For the prolonged possession of power corrupts its users. Yet the dictator, whose power is total, is permanent boss. He tolerates around him only collaborating yes men. As a result, hypocrisy flourishes, character perishes, and freedom dies.

To prove to its own subjects and to the world that it is popular, the dictatorship stages elections. But a 10 or 20 or 30 per cent antigovernment vote in those elections would indicate the existence of an opposition and the desire for an opposition party. The elections must therefore be unanimous. So, in Hitler Germany practically everybody voted

"Ja." In the Soviet Union, according to official data, over 99 per cent of the ballots are cast for the government. One hundred million people do not agree on anything. They would not agree that telephones are necessary, that bathing is healthy, that bread is good. They would certainly not all vote for Stalin unless they were afraid not to.

The terror is the decisive fact in a dictatorship, and the Soviet terror has become worse each year. This is the law of totalitarianism: it becomes more totalitarian.

"We have a very ancient democracy with a great sense of humor," said British Home Secretary James C. Ede. But a dictatorship never relaxes to smile; it lives on tensions. It needs enemies because enemies are an excuse for tension and terror. If enemies are lacking it creates them and inflates them.

Mrs. Franklin D. Roosevelt, who is the most gandhian figure among American political leaders, was arguing about human rights with Soviet Deputy Foreign Minister Andrei Vishinsky at a United Nations session in 1946. She asked, "Are we as individual nations so weak that we are going to forbid human beings to say what they think? . . . I am not always sure my government or my nation will be right. I hope it will be and I shall do my best to keep it as right as I can keep it." She therefore urged the United Nations to "consider what makes man more free; not governments but man."

In his reply to Mrs. Roosevelt, Vishinsky said, "We do not want to accept tolerance." That is the heart of the totalitarian's argument. The dictator can always justify intolerance; he recalls the sacrifices the people have made

to get as far as they have. But the truth is that a dictatorship does not want to be tolerant. It cannot afford to be
tolerant.

Is there any sign of dawning democracy in Soviet Russia?
Are there any free discussions within the Communist party?
There used to be until about 1929, and the discussions
were reported in the Soviet newspapers. Now there are
none. Is there any free speech, any criticism of the Soviet
government, of Stalin, or Soviet foreign policy? None at
all. Maybe Stalin is perfect and never makes mistakes.
Maybe the Soviet government always succeeds in what it
does and so no complaints are necessary. No. Stalin and a
few other top leaders have at times reversed policies and
admitted that things were going badly (collectivization,
for instance, in 1933), but then they blamed the little fellow who was carrying out their orders—often against his
better judgment—and their words unloosed a torrent of
condemnation of the little fellow. But this torrent is always dammed until the boss opens the sluice gates. Have
the trade unions more power? Do they launch strikes, or
engage in collective bargaining? No sign of it. Is there any
greater contact between Russia and the outside world, any
freer correspondence with foreigners, freer introduction of
foreign periodicals into Russia? Rather the contrary, there
is less.

The apologist for Sovietism could point to only one relaxation of restrictions: priests are less persecuted; the
Church can now establish religious seminaries and publish
literature. The atheistic Bolshevik regime is favoring the
unreformed Greek Orthodox Church. Democracy? No, just

the opposite. Official disfavor had, until a few years ago, saved the Russian Church from being chained to the government's chariot. Now the Kremlin is using the Church for nationalistic propaganda purposes abroad and at home; the Czar did the same thing. The Russian Church has been state-ified. The Soviet government has swallowed the last popular institution of the country. The government's domination of life has become total.

Marx and Lenin declared that after the owning class had been liquidated and the working class taken power, the state would wither away. The Russian state, however, far from withering, has blossomed into ubiquitous potency. Today, a new upper class, which directs the state and the means of production, exploits the working population. The discrepancy between the way the highest paid and the lowest paid in the Soviet Union live is greater than in any capitalist country. Stalin has nurtured an aristocracy which serves as his managerial bureaucracy and lives well at the expense of the masses, but has no power; the power is his and he shares it with the secret police.

The Soviet Union is a model despotism.

Those who love freedom fear the omnipotent state.

For them the state is not the end. The state is only the means. Man is the end.

People often hope that Stalin's death will make a difference and perhaps be conducive to democracy in Russia. But Stalin is dictator because a dictatorship needs men like Stalin.

All of Stalin's aides and possible successors are Stalinists. Nobody who wasn't could be in the front rank of dictatorship. Every possible successor to Stalin has by this time divested himself of the last ounce of Gandhiism. The firmly rooted Soviet system would not tolerate Gandhiism.

Might not a rising standard of living in Russia make for more democracy? A rising standard of living would be regarded by the leaders as proof of the virtue of the present system and they would teach that to the people.

A parallel is frequently suggested between the French and the Soviet revolutions: "The French Revolution had its terror and then it ushered in a long era of freedom."

Analogies may mislead. Historic analogies usually omit considerations of the changes time has wrought. Dialectic thinking based on constant change is much better than analogous thinking.

The French and the American revolutions marked the emergence of the bourgeoisie, the new industrial and trading class that wanted liberation from feudal masters. It was a propertied class and had the power to assert its will over the rest of the population and the government. It was the government.

The present, however, is the day of the highly centralized, aggrandized state, so mighty—in Nazi Germany and Soviet Russia, for instance—that it can crush some classes and dominate those that remain.

The French Revolution moved under the slogan "Liberty, Equality, Fraternity."

Russia's despotism is called liberty by her leaders, so liberty has slim chances. Kremlin spokesmen scoff at equality as a "bourgeois prejudice." And fraternity is the relationship between Russia and Finland, between Stalin and the millions in concentration camps, between the general in gold epaulets and the private in coarse uniform.

To repose hope in a parallel between the 1940's and the 1700's is wishful. It is based on the fallacy that any country, even a country as big as Russia, is an island. If Europe and Asia succumb to dictatorship, the likelihood of the dismantling of the dictatorship in Russia will be diminished. The twentieth century will then be confirmed as the Century of Dictators. If, on the other hand, democracy can firmly entrench itself throughout the non-Soviet world, the Soviet world may gradually, over many years, grow more democratic.

The expectation that death or insurrection will transform the Soviet government reflects a belief that others must ultimately accept our own system. We need merely sit, wait, and pray. But our democratic system is not perfect. It does not grant peace, security, plenty, or full freedom to all. If its content were enriched its survival would be guaranteed. Then its virtues would prove contagious. The future of democracy in Russia depends on the future of democracy outside Russia.

CHAPTER FIVE

WE ARE ALL VICTIMS

THOUGH imperialism is a form of dictatorship in
which the ruling foreigner holds the unwilling colony
in bondage, democracy may nevertheless exist in the colonies
of a democracy. It is a limited democracy, but only one who
has never tasted totalitarianism will deny that the British
gave India numerous liberties. Indian nationalist parties,
leaders, and newspapers have continually criticized, attacked and seriously inconvenienced the British government
—even in wartime. A tiny fraction of such activity in any
totalitarian regime would have cost them their lives.

The British government has imprisoned thousands of
Indians who committed no act of violence and no crime
other than that of hurling words at British policy. Incar-
ceration for political views is an inexcusable torment. Yet
with few exceptions the prisoners were allowed to leave
their jails and resume twisting the lion's tail. It is possible
to fight a democratic government and survive. This is not
true of a dictatorship.

I make these remarks apropos of Gandhi's declarations
about the Jews of Hitler Germany. . . . Shortly before I
flew to India from New York in 1946, Dr. Judah L.
Magnes, Chancellor of the Hebrew University of Jeru-

47

salem, called my attention to a letter he had written to Gandhi in 1938; he had never received a reply.

In his letter, Magnes, acknowledging himself a disciple of Gandhi, referred to an article in *Harijan* in which the Mahatma advised the Jews of Germany to offer Satyagraha, or nonviolent opposition, "to the godless fury of their dehumanized oppressors."

"I would challenge Hitler to shoot me or cast me into the dungeon," Gandhi wrote in his article. "I would not wait for fellow Jews to join me in civil resistance, but would have confidence that in the end the rest are bound to follow my example. . . . Suffering voluntarily undergone will bring them an inner strength and joy."

Magnes rejected Gandhi's idea. "The slightest sign of resistance," he wrote, "means killing or concentration camps or being done away with otherwise. It is usually in the dead of night that they are spirited away," Magnes recalled. "No one except their terrified families is the wiser. It makes not even a ripple on the surface of German life. The streets are the same, business goes on as usual, the casual visitor sees nothing. Contrast this with a single hunger strike in an American or English prison, and the public commotion that this arouses."

Magnes had put his finger on an essential difference between dictatorship and democracy. He hoped I would get a chance to mention the matter to Gandhi.

It came up the first day I spent with Gandhi at Dr. Mehta's Nature Cure Clinic at Poona. He mentioned the Hindu-Moslem riots then proceeding in the city of Ahmedabad. He said, "The trouble is that one side begins stabbing and killing, and then the other side does likewise. If one side let themselves be killed the trouble would end. But I cannot persuade them to be nonviolent. It is the same in Palestine. The Jews have a good case. I told Sidney Silverman (British Labor Member of Parliament) that the Jews have a good case in Palestine. If the Arabs have a claim to Palestine the Jews have a prior claim. Jesus was a Jew—the finest flower of Judaism. You can see that from the four stories that have come to us from the four disciples. They had untutored minds. They told the truth about Jesus. But Paul was not a Jew. He was a Greek. He had an oratorical mind, a dialectic mind, and he distorted Jesus. Jesus had a great force, the love force. But Christianity was perverted when it became the religion of kings at the time of Constantine. Then there were the Crusades and Peter the Hermit who persuaded the Christians to butcher the Saracens. The Moors were literally pushed into the sea. Christianity became barbarism. It remained so throughout the Middle Ages."

"And now?" I asked.

"Now," he replied, "Christianity sits on top of the cloud emitted by the atomic bomb. Nevertheless, compared to Christianity, Judaism is obstinate and unenlightened. I have heard Rabbi Hertz in London. He was a great orator. But he was constantly making excuses for the Jews. I have gone more frequently to Christian churches in South Africa and elsewhere than to synagogues. I understand Christianity better. But, as I told you, the Jews have a good case in Palestine."

I said, "Did you ever receive a letter, back in 1938 or

1939, from Dr. Judah Magnes, President of the Hebrew University of Jerusalem? He wrote it after you had made a statement urging the Jews of Germany to practice passive resistance against Hitler."

"I don't remember the letter," Gandhi confessed, "but I remember my own statement. I did not urge passive resistance. That is the wrong term. Many years ago, in South Africa, I spoke at a large public meeting presided over by Herman Kallenbach, a rich Jew of Johannesburg. I lived at his house often and formed an attachment for him. He introduced me as the champion of passive resistance. I stood up and said I did not believe in passive resistance. Satyagraha is something very active. It is the reverse of passive. Submission is passive and I dislike submission. The Jews of Germany made the mistake of submitting to Hitler."

"Magnes," I said, "argued in his letter to you that the Jews could do nothing else."

"Hitler," Gandhi solemnly affirmed, "killed five million Jews. It is the greatest crime of our time. But the Jews should have offered themselves to the butcher's knife. They should have thrown themselves into the sea from cliffs. I believe in hara-kiri. I do not believe in its militaristic connotations, but it is a heroic method."

"You think," I said, "that the Jews should have committed collective suicide?"

"Yes," Gandhi agreed, "that would have been heroism. It would have aroused the world and the people of Germany to the evils of Hitler's violence, especially in 1938, before the war. As it is they succumbed anyway in their millions."

When I reported this conversation to Dr. Magnes, he said, "It may be that Gandhi is right in thinking that if the Jews had committed suicide they might have impressed the world more deeply than the loss of six million lives has done. Yet I do not see how in the world such an action would be physically possible. The few hundred in the Fortress of Massada were able to commit suicide because they were in a confined place and were up against a belligerent army. How could six million or one million or one hundred thousand do anything of the sort? And if they had, would the impression on the world be any more lasting than the annihilation of the six million has been?

Mahatma Gandhi has never lived under a thoroughly totalitarian regime; his generosity and humanity make it difficult for him to realize how very cruel a dictatorship can be. In India, and in Palestine, and other places, violence or organized nonviolence is a form of "public relations." When they wish to influence policy, Americans, Englishmen, Frenchmen, or Swedes lobby, wire, write, vote, march, strike. In colonial Asia the protesters, whose votes cannot make policy, riot, stab, shoot, loot. The purpose of the protesters is to change British policy, which, on occasions, they have succeeded in doing. Disturbances in the East excite reactions in London, in Parliament, in the press, in the political parties, and in churches. The government is put under such terrific pressure that it must answer its critics publicly and, at times, alter its strategy.

Thus gandhian nonviolence as well as its ugly opposite—Zionist terror—implies the existence of a free democratic society in England (and in America). It is to this court of public opinion that the resisters in India and kidnappers in Palestine have appealed. But suppose there were no democracy in Western nations?

A British prime minister could not order a million people dragged out of their houses and off the streets to be melted down to soap in fiery furnaces. Hitler could—and did.

Genêt, a celebrated foreign correspondent, writes in the *New Yorker*:

Before the Nazi war, there were a hundred thousand Jews living in Amsterdam. Today, there are five thousand. Catching Jews here was easy. The Gestapo merely cut the bridges of the canals leading to the Jewish neighborhoods they called ghettos, flushed the inmates out of their little eighteenth-century houses, shot those who tried to escape from what had suddenly become fatal racial islands, tagged the marooned remainder with yellow Stars of David, and carted them off in cattle cars to the Fatherland's concentration camps. Of Holland's hundred and forty thousand Jews, a hundred and fourteen thousand perished under the Germans . . .

How could the victims of such mass barbarism oppose it? Not the immediate, unhappy victims, but all mankind must practice active resistance to dictatorship, for we are all its victims. Its spirit touches us even when its hands cannot.

Gandhi's ideas of democracy and Gandhi himself could not survive in a dictatorship. A dictator would simply order Mr. Gandhi removed into oblivion. Nobody would ever hear of him again. Suppose half a million defied the dictatorship out of solidarity with Gandhi. They would be liquidated. Suppose three million defied the dictatorship. They would be liquidated. Suppose twenty million Indians defied the dictatorship. With twenty million crusading

Gandhians in any country the dictatorship would never be established in the first place. Nations that are true to the fundamental tenets of Gandhiism will escape the tortures of totalitarianism. Gandhiism does not mix with Hitlerism or Stalinism.

CHAPTER SIX

SUNDAY MORNING IN DÜSSELDORF

THE momentous question of our day is whether people who have once fallen under the spell and heel of a totalitarian regime will, when released, resist it or succumb to it again. Have Germans, Italians, and Japanese been "cured" forever of an inclination toward dictators? Or will the emotions, beliefs, and conditions which led them to favor and submit to one dictatorship make them the easy victims of a second?

The sun went up "like thunder" over the ruined houses of the city of Düsseldorf in the British zone in Germany. I looked out of the window of my room in the Park Hotel. Most buildings on the horizon had disintegrated, under the bombs, into mounds of dirt or jagged half-walls and jagged quarter-walls with many unframed window holes.

Downstairs my car was waiting. The chauffeur was a German from Stettin, hard working and silent except when I asked questions. For sustenance he had several thick slices of brown, soggy bread. He fought in the Reichswehr in Holland, France, Russia, Crimea, and the Caucasus, in Greece, and in Germany on the western front. Conditions in Russia, he said, are primitive; it will take them fifty years to catch up with Europe. He liked the Dutch most; they are clean. When the Russians entered Stettin, they tried to rape his eighteen-year-old sister. She committed suicide. Then his mother did the same. He said this with cold matter-of-factness, in the same tone as a Jewish woman said to me in London: "My parents? Yes. They were put into the furnace at Auschwitz." Europe has lived through too much to be emotional; people have no tears left. You cannot be emotional and live in a city of ruins.

I drove to the central railway station. It had been hit several times. A wooden ceiling had been built in under the bombed permanent ceiling of the main waiting room. At the left end of the waiting room was a beer keller. A man in topcoat and felt hat stopped me when I tried to enter. I had to buy a ticket. A Communist party election campaign meeting was in progress. Tickets were a mark apiece. I had only a fifty-mark bill. He had no change. I offered him a Chesterfield instead. He said, "Fine. There I make a five-mark profit." An American cigarette fetches from six to nine marks on the black market.

The beer keller was about sixty yards long and twenty wide. It was half above and half below the pavement level. Four electric bulbs cast some rays of light on the dimness. The audience consisted of some two hundred men and ten women, seated at round tables. Most of the men and women were middle-aged; nobody looked less than forty. A bald, gray-haired, frail waiter in white jacket tiptoed from table to table dispensing tumblers of beer from a platter.

The well-dressed speaker, a physician, said, "Twenty-five per cent of all German physicians joined the Nazi party."

I turned over the folder on which I was taking
announced this morning's meeting as one of the :
dorf Middle Class." At the entrance I had been h.n   d a
thin-paper Communist election leaflet entitled *Little Nazi,
What Now?* It read: "There were 12 million members of
the Nazi party of Germany. Men, women, and youth,
hundreds of thousands of them were forced either by moral
pressure or the fear of losing their jobs to enter the ranks
of the Nazi party. . . . Shall all these 12 million now be
thrown into the same pot?" The leaflet urged "little Nazis"
to join the Communist party.

"We can clearly predict," the doctor continued, "that
catastrophe is inevitable unless we follow the teachings of
Marxism. It is significant that the American statesman,
Byrnes, said in his recent speech that the catastrophe which
overtook Germany after 1919 could have been avoided if
the Germans had taken the advice of Karl Liebknecht."

"Communists want planned science," he said a moment
later. "That is socialism. The Nazis had a plan and an
organization, for instance in aviation and medicine. Then
what is the difference between socialism and Nazism? The
Nazi goal was destruction and collapse. Socialism in Russia,
on the other hand, is making fascinating researches in history, medicine, in all sciences. I recently read an American
book on the atom. The authors oppose the use of atomic
energy for civilian purposes. America wants atomic energy
only for militarism and diplomatic pressure. In the U.S.A.,
atomic energy means retrogression, stop, restraint. In the
U.S.S.R., it means scientific advance and benefit to humanity."

discussed the German youth and education. "The of the German physician," he warned, "must be democratized, otherwise reaction will flourish again. The intellectuals must side with the workers, for how can physicians be prosperous unless the working class is prosperous? Many German intellectual leaders, for instance, Scharnhorst, Clausewitz, Fichte, and so on, opposed the Junkers. In 1848, many intellectuals supported the revolution. In the American Civil War, over eight hundred thousand German forty-eighters, among them thirty-seven generals, fought on the side of progress.

"Socialism wants peace. Under socialism, women, who now experience difficulty getting into medical schools, would have no difficulty.

"I must finish. We will either move toward progress or disappear under atomic bombs."

Handclapping rewarded the speaker as he rushed to the door. I ran after him and caught him in the station waiting room. I asked him his name. "Dr. Karl Hagedorn."

I said I was an American journalist and had come to Germany to see the effect of Nazism on Germans. "You quoted Secretary of State Byrnes," I said, "as declaring that Germany might have avoided collapse by following Liebknecht. Now I would be surprised if Byrnes had ever heard of Karl Liebknecht. But if he has he certainly would not think that Germany should have taken the advice of a Communist leader. Byrnes is a conservative."

"Ja," the doctor said with a sigh, "then who could it have been? I read it in the press."

"Byrnes has made one speech on Germany recently, at

Stuttgart," I recalled, "and you will not find your reference in it. I can remember no such statement. In the second place, you affirmed that America would not use atomic energy for industrial purposes whereas Russia would. You are wrong about the United States. It would be quite unlike Americans not to try to use atomic energy in industry. As a matter of fact, work along this line is proceeding. And as to Russia, how do you know? This is a deep Soviet secret, and you know nothing about atomic activities in Russia. Neither does any other outsider."

He stood in front of me, silent.

I said, "Germany has had twelve years of the lying propaganda of Goebbels. One would think that Germans had had enough. But here you are doing exactly what Goebbels did."

He said nothing and looked uncomfortable. I turned and went back into the meeting place.

Later, I walked out into the street. Ruined walls were plastered with political posters. The several German parties expressed their views. A Christian Democratic Union (CDU) poster read, THE CHRISTIAN VOTES CDU. Right next to each CDU poster, the Social Democratic party had put up a rival poster, THE TRUE CHRISTIAN IS A SOCIALIST. VOTE SPD.

The Socialists appealed to the women of Germany to help raise the morale of the youth. The CDU cried, "No War Anymore." Only the Communists made promises. "Do You Want More Coal? Vote Communist." But coal production and distribution were completely in the hands of the foreign occupying powers and no German party, whether Socialist or Communist or anything, could give more coal to German voters. "Do You Want Prices Reduced? Vote Communist." But prices, and wages, were fixed by the occupying armies when they marched into Germany, fixed at Nazi, wartime levels. Germans could not raise or lower prices.

Quack doctors and quack politicians trade on the credulity of persons in pain. Gullible people can neither see nor hear; they can only swallow. Astrologers, fortunetellers, Messiahs, fake "Christs," mystic cults, charlatans, as well as Communists and Fascists, flourish in times of turmoil, uncertainty, and misery.

A dictator's deadliest weapon is terror. Terror creates fear which intensifies the desire for security and the readiness to pay for it with character. The gods of a dictatorship demand human sacrifices, and the greatest of these is character. Terror transforms men into hypocrites who lie, confess, and grovel in order to succeed and live. Terror breeds bandwagon riders, boot lickers, cynics, and sycophants.

A dictatorship builds itself up as an awesome, thousand-year monolithic giant which no individual can change or weaken. So why try? Conspiracy is folly in view of ubiquitous informers and towering fright. Hence complacency, passivity, and a play-the-game psychology. The same hero who is ready to die for his country on the battlefield is a civilian coward. He sees no chance of success and only the certainty that his attack on the citadel of totalitarianism would drag himself, his family, and friends to death without achieving anything except an intensification of repression.

Dictatorship weakens will power. It discourages thought: thoughts are dangerous. It discourages political initiative; all wisdom and authority spout from the brow of the dictator. In these circumstances the individual adopts the protective color of gray and tries to merge with the crowd. Excessive ambition is a death warrant. A popular general courts danger. He who differs courts danger. There is a premium on docility, acquiescence, self-effacement, and obedience. These are the best guaranty of safety.

Youth soon learns this lesson. School and incessant, clanging propaganda explain it all as a necessary and glorious service to the state in the name of the flowering of the nation, the triumph of the revolution, and the happiness of future generations. The strident, hard-working homeland is lauded and compared favorably with the decadent, collapsing democracies. Access to the democracies is strictly limited lest this balloon of official lies be pricked.

When outside pressure laid low the dictatorships of Germany, Italy, and Japan, the ground was littered with the debris of broken individuals. Human pygmies with shriveled characters hunted in the ruins. The new masters met no resistance. The capacity to resist had been killed by the dictators. Only a few fanatics remained in isolated spots.

Perhaps these countries were always docile and disciplined and therefore succumbed to the dictator who made them still more so. As soon as the dictatorship crumbles, the totalitarianized sheep, or at least some of them, can readily be directed into a new totalitarian pen. In Germany, Italy, Hungary, and many other European countries, numerous Fascists have joined the Communist parties.

The process of de-totalitarianization is, first of all, a matter of restoring character and human dignity. It is a matter of reinforcing the gandhian ideas of scrupulous regard for means, higher respect for man, and individual or popular initiative as distinguished from government enactment. The negative formula of excommunicating Nazis and other Fascists is often necessary. But they may jump on another totalitarian bandwagon. Some have. In any case, denazification affects only those who are brown enough to be recognized. What about the brown, or black, or red that entered the blood and soul in small quantities? This needs a gandhian antidote. "Denazify with Gandhi," might be an appropriate prescription.

The shreds of individuality cannot be sewed together with a bayonet; nor can democracy be restored according to the Biblical injunction of an "eye for an eye" which, in the end, would make everybody blind.

Any attempt to introduce democracy or to check totalitarianism must constantly emphasize the rehabilitation of personality. Freedom and responsibility help. Rigid authority hinders.

Acute physical suffering also reduces democratic respect for means. General Lucius D. Clay, American Military Governor in Germany, said he thought the Germans would not go Communist but he would not vouch for it if the daily ration fell from 1,550 to 1,250 calories. In Europe, the difference between a democrat and a Communist may be half a loaf of bread per day or a hundredweight of coal per month.

Spiritual regeneration—without which democracy will

perish—is not facilitated by hunger, clubs, curbs, or an authoritarian state.

Dictatorship irritates the people. Millions nevertheless get used to it. With the passing of years, millions forget what freedom is. In Russia, the new generation never knew freedom and so its opinion on freedom is worthless.

The remnants of Fascism in the ex-dictatorships are potential recruits for a new Fascism or for Communism. On the other hand, totalitarianism cannot help but produce a revulsion against compulsion and a thirst for relaxation and liberty, a desire to be left alone. The collapse of a dictatorship therefore presents an exciting opportunity for democracy. It is important to punish the criminals and watch the backsliders. It is infinitely more important to use every possible positive measure by which the ex-slaves can be shown how to become free men.

General Lucius D. Clay believes that the American administration in Germany ought to be civilian. A military administration, by its very nature, perpetually emphasizes the fact of outside compulsion. People then tend to react to it as to a dictatorship. That frame of mind would not be conducive to democracy.

Democracy can only be implanted by democrats in a democratic way. I would try treating the ex-enemy and all antidemocrats as patients rather than as criminals. Many are criminals. They are criminals because they are sick. Hate and force have been used so much in our world. We might try kindness. We might try democracy.

In an interview on June 20, 1947, Lord Pakenham, British Minister in Charge of Germany, said, "To any good will that I have shown them the Germans have always responded in equal measure." Such treatment is based on a good pedagogic principle and on the ideas of Christ and Gandhi.

Our world, which threatens to slip into totalitarianism, is in much greater danger from an effort to perpetuate slavery in ex-enemy countries, in colonies, and in the democracies than from a brave experiment in freedom. To succeed, those who conduct the experiment must themselves be free men, rich in dignity and rich in character.

CHAPTER SEVEN

HITLER AND STALIN

TO SERVE his demagogic purposes, Mussolini used to call his regime "proletarian." The Soviet system is officially the "dictatorship of the proletariat." Its spokesmen also speak of it as "Bolshevik," "Communist," and "Socialist" interchangeably. Hitler's dictatorship was "National Socialist" or, in German abbreviation, Nazi. But Stalin has said in several public utterances that the "Hitlerites," as he prefers to call them, were not nationalist, they were imperialist, and they were not socialist, they were reactionary. During the war, the Soviet embassy in London therefore tried to dissuade the BBC from saying "Nazi," and, in 1947, Soviet diplomats objected to the use of "National Socialist." For Stalin had declared that Soviet culture was "national in form, and Socialist in content." Stalin also claims that he has established "socialism in one country," or national socialism.

The similarity does not end with the names. Dictatorships resemble one another in ruthless methods, in cruelty to persons, and in disregard of life. Before he was in office Hitler promised that "heads would roll," and many did. The Kremlin has drawn a bloody trail across the length and breadth of Russia. Foreign Communists often speak with great gusto in private about whom they will shoot when they get power; such talk must satisfy something in them that is not normal.

When he was Bolshevik Number Two, Trotsky wrote a book justifying terror; Stalin has taken every page out of that book. Violence is the way of the minority that cannot convince the majority. The ax, the revolver, the castor oil are the religion of those who have no faith in ideas, no morality, and no love of man—though they preach the welfare of mankind.

Violence begins as a means to an end, and then it devours the original end and becomes a technique whereby power may be brutally maintained.

In the early years of the Bolshevik Revolution, the secret police was a weapon against the enemies of the regime. When the capitalists, kulaks, the counterrevolutionists had been liquidated, the secret police turned against those people who had brought about the revolution and were still loyal to it. Loyalty was their crime.

At its inception, Bolshevism was sharply distinguished from Fascism. The old, early Bolsheviks were intellectuals, workers, or professional revolutionists, like Lenin, Trotsky, and Stalin, whose first interest lay with the working class. The Nazis were, for the most part, middle-class adventurers and politically displaced persons who collaborated with industrialists and Junkers against the working class.

The Bolsheviks drank deeply at the fountain of the French Revolution and of west-European liberal philosophers. Czarist autocracy was repugnant to them. So was the Church which served the absolute monarchs. Democracy and liberty, therefore, were not foreign ideals to Lenin and Trotsky. They promised that the state would "wither away" and then the people would be free. No Fascist ever dreamed such beautiful dreams. Fascist dictatorship would be permanent; for "a thousand years," Hitler predicted.

The Bolsheviks, moreover, were internationalists. Internationalism and hostility to nationalism, imperialism, and racism were the warp and woof of Leninist Communism. Since Communism wanted "the workers of the world to unite," how could it discriminate against or in favor of anybody on account of blood, place of birth, color, or creed of parents? It judged persons by their economic pursuits and their social origin.

The Nazis, on the other hand, urged the doctrine of racial and national superiority: "Deutschland Über Alles;" "Aryan Supremacy;" "One Reich, One Folk, One Fuehrer," all Germans must be brought under one national dictatorship. Herein were the seeds of the Second World War.

Mussolini began his career as a Socialist, a left-wing Socialist. Then he accepted nationalism, and erected a dictatorship. That made him a Fascist.

State control over all capital, plus secret-police dictatorship, plus nationalism are national socialism even though its leaders speak in the name of the proletariat. There are all kinds of socialism. Karl Marx called antisemitism "the socialism of fools." National socialism is the socialism of criminals.

In Russia, today, the old terminology remains: Bolshevism, Communism, and Socialism. But the abandonment of democratic goals, the mounting rigors of dictatorship, and the introduction of nationalism make Stalin the ideological brother of Hitler and Mussolini.

The parting of ways in Russia apparently came in 1934 and 1935. Stalin knew that Soviet economy had not yet fulfilled the promise of plenty, and would not for quite a time. Something had to be added to stimulate zeal and faith. He might add democracy to the state-capitalistic economic forms and get real socialism. Or he could add nationalism. In characteristic fashion he experimented with both. He put democracy on paper in a new constitution. Simultaneously he began introducing nationalism.

But a dictatorship finds it difficult to abdicate. Nor could Mr. Stalin afford to relax restrictions on personal freedom when dissatisfaction with material conditions might arise. On the contrary, he had to tighten the restrictions and seek high-ranking scapegoats for the regime's failures. They were the defendants at the Moscow trials. The trials and purges of 1935, 1936, 1937, and 1938 canceled the constitution and killed every last vestige of democracy in the Communist party, in the trade unions, and in the country. What remains in Russia today is a state that owns and works all capital, that rules despotically, and that teaches and practices nationalism. This is an ominous combination.

The Soviet Union is the home of numerous nationalities. Great Russians constitute about 54 per cent of the population. There are some forty million Ukrainians. And there are Armenians, Georgians, Kalmucks, Uzbeks, Tajiks, Jews, Buriats, Ossets, Kabardians, White Russians, Azerbaijani, Germans, Moldavians, Tatars, Adjari, Abkhas, Circassians, etc., etc.—more than one hundred and twenty in all.

The Czar's government was a government of Great (flaxen-haired, blue-eyed) Russians who were contemptuous of non-Russians. It tried to russify them in language, dress, customs, and religion. Until 1917, Russia was a prison house of national minorities. The Bolshevik Revolution undertook to convert it into a league of free, equal nations. All the national minorities were encouraged by the Soviets to speak their own tongues and if those tongues had no grammar or written script, Moscow sent scientists to develop them. In areas inhabited by the minorities, separate republics or subrepublics were set up with officials who were members of those minorities. This amounted to provincial or regional autonomy.

Before the revolution, and even after it, some Communists had opposed this line. They called it nationalism. They said it stressed racial differences and would prevent the emergence of a new person, product of the revolution, who was neither a Russian nor Armenian, who was a class-conscious, devoted Soviet citizen, an internationalist.

But the Kremlin decided that it had to reverse the Czar's policy of Russians First. It had to give the half of the Soviet Union that was not Russian a sense of belonging and ruling. Georgians like Stalin and Ordzhonikidze, Armenians like Mikoyan and Karakhan, Jews like Zinoviev, Kamenev, Litvinov, and Kaganovich rose to the top rung of the Soviet hierarchy where their presence was concrete proof that discrimination against non-Russians had ended. Jews, once the objects of cruel pogroms and other forms of anti-semitic persecution, received protection, as did other racial groups.

All Bolsheviks and even the most anti-Soviet foreign observers stated that the Communist revolution had solved the problem of national minorities. The absence of racial discrimination was hailed as one of the greatest achievements of the Soviet system.

When the smoke—and propaganda—of the Second World War had cleared from the skies over Russia, wide cracks were revealed in this Soviet edifice of interracial amity. Documents and data emanating direct from the Kremlin showed that during the war Stalin—in violation of the 1936 Stalin constitution—had suppressed the autonomous republics of the Kalmucks located on the Volga between Stalingrad and Astrakhan, of the Tatars in the Crimea, and of the Chechen and Ingushi in the North Caucasus. All these peoples are Moslems. Their territories were invaded by the Nazi army; they were, apparently, disloyal to the Soviets and collaborated with Hitler. It is known that many of them fought for Germany on the Western Front; some were captured by the American army. Many thousands of Kalmuck and other deserters are now in camps in the American and British zones of Germany. They may be settled eventually in Arab countries in the Near East.

A clue to the origins of interracial friction in Soviet Russia is found in *The Bolshevik*, the official "theoretical and political journal of the Communist party of the Soviet Union." The July 1945 issue contains an article by G. Alexandrov, chief of the party's department of political education. Alexandrov complains that:

our historians do not adequately analyze the domestic history of the various peoples of the Soviet Union. The class war of the nationality is consequently glossed over, and certain feudal leaders and princes become national heroes. As an example, it is possible to take the publication in Kazan of the epic, "Eadegay." Towards the end of 1940, there appeared in the Tatar magazine *Soviet Edebiati* a summarized rendering of the "Eadegay" epic prepared for publication by the Tatar writer, N. Isanbet. The hero of the "Eadegay" epic began to be popular as a hero of the Tatar nation.

Eadegay was one of the great feudals of the Golden Horde, a prominent military commander and leader, follower of Takhtamish and Tamerlane, and, later, emir of the Golden Horde. He made devastating raids on Russian cities and villages. It is known that in 1408 Eadegay led a Tatar-Mongol pogrom-invasion against Moscow, burned Nizhni-Novgorod, Pereyaslav, Rostov, Serpukhov, and many cities near Moscow, levied a tribute on Moscow, sacked Ryazan on his return march, and deported thousands of Russians as slaves.

In other words, Eadegay behaved like a Tatar khan of the fifteenth century who fought the Muscovite Great Russians. Eadegay certainly cannot serve as a model for a good citizen of any country. But neither can Alexander Nevsky, who was a Russian knight of the thirteenth century, nor Ivan the Terrible, nor Peter the Great, nor Catherine the Great, nor General Suvarov, who fought wars and suppressed revolutions throughout Europe in the eighteenth century. Yet beginning in 1936, the Kremlin took these tyrants and marauders out of the dustbin of history to which the early Bolsheviks properly consigned them, brushed them off, gave them some thick Soviet paint, and offered them as the new heroes of the Soviet Union.

"Then why," the Tatars asked, "cannot we in 1940 do the same with our national heroes?"

"No," said Moscow. "Eadegay defeated the Russians." "Eadegay" was prohibited.

Thus Russian nationalism begot Tatar nationalism and Russian discrimination against Tatars.

An even worse situation has arisen in the Ukraine. There have always been nationalistic, even separatistic tendencies among Ukrainian Communists and non-Communists. Several times in the 1920's and 1930's, the Kremlin announced purges and punishments of Ukrainians who favored secession from the Soviet Union. When Moscow began fostering Russian nationalism the effect was to strengthen Ukrainian nationalism. During their occupation of the Ukraine, the Nazis did what they could to reinforce Ukrainian hopes of a Ukraine independent of Moscow.

To insure itself of the loyalty of the Ukrainian people, Moscow has boasted that it incorporated into the Ukraine all the areas of Poland, Czechoslovakia, and Rumania inhabited by Ukrainians, thereby fulfilling "a thousand-year-old Ukrainian dream." Stalin brought all the Ukrainian lands of Europe under the Soviet flag; how then could the Ukrainians wish to secede from the Soviet Union?

To strengthen further the bonds between the Ukraine and Moscow, the Soviet regime, in recent years, has been glorifying Bogdan Khmelnitski, a Ukrainian hetman and national hero. During the war, an important military decoration was created in the name of Bogdan Khmelnitski, and the city of Pereyaslav was renamed Pereyaslav-Khmelnitski.

The point is that in January 1654, Khmelnitski united the Ukraine with Russia, and Moscow wants to stress this fact. Now, say "Khmelnitski" to a Jew who lived in Russia in the czarist era. His immediate response will be "Pogroms." Bogdan Khmelnitski is known for his massacres of Jews.

Ukrainian nationalism, today too strong to be suppressed, has always meant antisemitism.

For the first time since the Bolshevik Revolution of 1917, moreover, evidence is available of official antisemitism which takes the form, for instance, of the rapid elimination of Jews from the Soviet foreign service and the curtailment of the number of Jews who may attend certain educational institutions, notably the school for diplomats in Moscow. Hundreds of Jews used to work in the Soviet Ministry of Foreign Affairs in Moscow. Now there are only a handful. The same trend is visible in other branches of the government. The bulk of the Jewish members of the Communist party, moreover have, according to reliable reports, left that organization.

These developments were inevitable when the Kremlin sponsored Great Russian nationalism, when Stalin could say at a banquet in Moscow, on May 24, 1945, that the Russians were the "leading nation of the Soviet Union." This is the old doctrine of Russians First, of the supremacy of one race; its corollary is the inferiority of other races.

Pan-Slavism, Pan-Germanism, and Pan-Nipponism are brother theories. They involve discrimination at home and expansion abroad.

Nationalistic frictions inside Russia are a recent growth and have not yet caught up with many foreigners. But the minorities in the Soviet Union, notably certain groups of

Moslems and Ukrainians, reacted against Great Russian nationalism during the war.

For the hundred and more racial non-Russian and non-Slav minorities, the Russian nationalism, which Stalin, the Georgian, assiduously cultivated after 1935, served to intensify the irritation which Muscovite dictatorship had always excited. The minorities enjoyed wide cultural autonomy; but in economic and political matters their paper autonomy was canceled out by the Kremlin's rigid centralization. There is no more centralized government in the world than the Soviet Union's. The federal authorities are in direct charge of the economy of the entire country. The so-called autonomous republics of the minorities obey Moscow. This has its virtues; it permits national planning and co-ordination of effort. But it kills local initiative and independence. An omnipotent federal government has made a mockery of Soviet federalism.

In some future United States of Europe or in a federated India or a unified Asia, a compromise will be necessary between the centralized government and the governments of the various states, provinces, and national units. But dictatorship, whether Hitlerite or Stalinist, whether Fascist or Communist, excludes such a compromise. It monopolizes power at the center to the detriment of the periphery.

The combination of dictatorship and nationalism has destroyed the early internationalism of Soviet domestic and foreign policies. At the United Nations and in other conferences, Soviet representatives now insist on "national sovereignty." Hence their objection to the American scheme for the control of the atomic bomb and to international co-

operation with a view to the economic revival of Europe.
Hence, too, Moscow's objection to the abolition of the veto
in the United Nations charter; the veto is the embodiment
of national sovereignty. Hence the Soviet's objection to
world government which their press regards as "reactionary."

Nationalism intensifies dictatorship, and dictatorship
heightens nationalism.

But nationalism, usually less pathological and explosive,
exists in all democracies. It is an element in their weakness.
It is also an element in the weakness of the democratic
world, for it produces division and hate.

Economic and political nationalism cause imperialism
and wars. They create color bars and racial discrimination.
They are un-Christian, undemocratic, immoral. Nationalism
is the curse of the modern world. "The end of Europe was
brought about by nationalism," says Professor Albert Ein-
stein.

Civilization may succumb to totalitarianism if nationalism continues to grow. It is growing. The humiliation and
misery of prolonged foreign rule have made too many Indians indocentric and added a feverish nationalism to their
fully justified desire for liberty. The young Zionist terror-
ists of Palestine are embryo Nazis. A Tory United States
senator, champion of a corrupt spoils system in politics and
symbol of everything that is decadent and unliberal in the
Southern states, publicly implies that an honored American
civil servant is less of an American because his parents were
born in Austro-Hungary more than three score and ten years
ago. Southern politicians openly preach "white supremacy"

and organize against Catholics, Negroes, and Jews. Egypt insists that foreigners declare their religion on entering and leaving the country. Moslems and Hindus fight; Hindus maltreat Untouchables; Jews and Arabs are at odds; Christians and Jews do not behave as brothers should. Czechoslovakia, once the most civilized democracy in Central Europe, has, under a Communist-led government, taken measures against Hungarians and Germans, apparently hoping thereby to become racially "pure" (whatever that means) and all-Slav.

This is how democracy dies. Cell by cell, fiber by fiber, nationalism transforms healthy democracy into malignant totalitarianism. The mounting virulence of postwar nationalism attacks a democratic system already seriously undermined by other circumstances, and the results are disastrous.

"All men are born equal" is the foundation of democracy. The foundation is undermined where a man is not equal because of the shape of his nose, the place of his birth, the color of his skin, the nature of his religion, accent of his speech, the "foreign" sound of his name, or the beliefs and deeds of his relatives. Only those who chose their parents have a right to persecute.

Persons who value their personal freedom and their lives must, in fighting Fascism and Communism, concentrate their fire on every manifestation of nationalism, racism, and class or caste snobbery. There is only one aristocracy, and its ranks are open to all of clean character and high morals who help their fellow men. Ample room is provided in it for politicians and diplomats. How many seek membership?

CHAPTER EIGHT

THE CHOICE

FORMER Vice-President Henry A. Wallace has said, "As between Fascism and Communism I prefer Communism." But both are fatal to freedom. If the world were indeed faced with the Fascism-or-Communism choice, democracy would be doomed.

Hitler and Goebbels narrowed the choice down to Nazism or Bolshevism; every anti-Nazi was a Communist. Hitler called President Benes a Bolshevik for wanting Czechoslovakia to remain independent.

Franco said, "Spain represents a choice between Fascism and Communism." During the Spanish civil war of 1936-39, many reactionaries used this argument to justify their support of Fascism.

Reaction frightens some people into the Communist camp. Communism frightens some people into the rightist camp. Each extreme is the recruiting agent of the other. Democracy suffers.

Greece is a terrible example.

For no sufficient reason, the Greek king was allowed to return to his throne in Athens. The rightist royalists rallied round him. The Communists, always first and always shrillest, cried Alarm and called on the men of the middle to join their antimonarchist standard. Since the danger of reaction was real, many did join. Thereupon the king's friends pointed to the growing Communist following and appealed to the more conservative moderates to support the king. Some did. This gave the Communists a new recruiting argument and they used it effectively. Communist success in turn spurred the royalists to pull another section of the middle into the extreme right camp.

If this process were to continue long enough, the entire middle would disappear and only the two extremes would remain. There could be no accommodation or bridge between them. They could only fight.

France, Italy, China, and many other lands, even the United States to a very slight degree, are threatened with this polarization of society. It is the greatest political peril to peace within the democratic world. A clash between expanded extremes in a whole series of countries threatens an international civil war and, perhaps, the third world war.

The prevention of war and the salvation of democracy lies in the reinforcement of the middle and the weakening of the reactionary and Communist extremes.

Both extremes always try to drive moderate contenders from the field. In a country like America the reactionaries feel that if they could only make it appear that Communism is a menace they alone can repel they would rule the roost. In a country like France, the Communists are confident of victory in single combat with the reactionaries. The French Communists accordingly proclaim that there is only one fight, against the reactionaries, and that all those who op-

pose reaction must consequently join the Communists. Each
extreme hopes to win by annihilating the middle and forcing a choice between itself and the opposite pole.

Sometimes, as in China, the Communists describe themselves as the middle, and as democrats. Their foreign
friends present them to a naive world as "agrarian reformers." They are that, and China needs a land reform
desperately, but the Chinese Communists are also a one-
party government, and they constantly volunteer approval
of Muscovite policy. If the Chinese Communists were accepted as the middle, no real middle would have a chance.

In Germany, before Hitler, the Communists often supported Nazi proposals aimed at weakening the republic.
Asked why, they explained that if the republic fell, the
Nazis would take office, fail, and succumb to the Communists. The extremes think of the road to power as leading
over the dead bodies of the moderate middle.

In pre-Hitler days, the Communists naturally concentrated their fire on the Social Democrats. Social Democrats
believe in socialism plus freedom; Communists advocate
socialism with dictatorship. As democrats, the German
Social Democrats were anti-Nazi, and for the same reason
they were anti-Communist. The Communists therefore
called them "Social Fascists"; Communists excel in mis-
leading vituperation. The bitterness between the Communists and Social Democrats helped put Hitler into power.

This terrible lesson and the threat of Fascism throughout
Europe brought about a United Front or Popular Front in
republican Spain, France, and other countries. Liberals,

Socialists, and Communists collaborated against Fascists. Moscow originated and fostered this co-operation.

In all such combinations, the Communists worked hardest and sacrificed most. But in every case, they sought to control the United or Popular Front, and frequently they were so successful that the collaboration ended in a "Never Again" determination on the part of the non-Communists.

The non-Communists discovered that the Communists lusted for power, stopped at nothing to get it, lied, and obeyed the Kremlin.

That Popular Front experience in the second half of the 'thirties died suddenly with the signing of the Stalin-Hitler pact of August 1939. How could anti-Nazis work with the followers of Stalin when Stalin was in close touch with the Nazis? How could Communists claim to be anti-Fascists when they sabotaged the war against Hitler in England, France, and America until he invaded Russia? Apparently, Communist "anti-Fascism" meant agreement with Russia even when it helped Fascists and even at the cost of the democracies.

Since then, the world has achieved a deeper understanding of the character of totalitarian policies and strategies. Totalitarians, red, brown, or black, are enemies of democracies. A truce with them is a loss of time and position. Anti-totalitarians cannot trust totalitarians and therefore cannot work with them. The presence of Communists in key positions is an insuperable obstacle to the unification of the trade-union, working-class, and liberal anti-Fascist movements in any one country or in the world, for millions of democrats will refuse to have anything to do with anti-democrats.

Decent persons may at times feel uncomfortable about rejecting the help of Communists in electing a fine candidate, fighting imperialism, combatting racial discrimination, getting more housing, etc., etc. But the Communists would be a means to an end, and a true democrat avails himself only of those means that are worthy of the end. Otherwise the transaction is immoral.

The implications of merged effort with totalitarians, or with corrupt politicians, are so far-reaching that they defeat the partial good that may be accomplished.

Socialists or liberals who work with Communists cannot attack Communism without exposing themselves to the charge of inconsistency. Communists want collaboration with Socialists, trade-unionists, and liberals in order to silence their natural foes and competitors. But unless Socialists, for instance, criticize and expose Communists as totalitarians, the public fails to understand the difference between democratic Socialists and Communists. In those circumstances, the richer resources, dynamic propaganda, and authoritarian discipline of the Communists brings them electoral success.

The Communists may supply non-Communists with large audiences, with radio programs, with publicity. The non-Communists pay a high price for these. During his famous speech in Madison Square Garden in New York, on September 12, 1946, Mr. Henry A. Wallace uttered some slight criticisms of Russian policy. The hall was packed with Communists, and they hissed. In the remainder of his

address, Wallace omitted the further unfavorable remarks
on Russia contained in the prepared text. Other speakers
addicted to Communist collaboration frequently attack
British and American policy in Greece, British deeds in
Palestine, etc. But they ignore the atrocities against persons
and against democracy which the Russians and Communists
constantly perpetrate in the Soviet sphere of influence. Here
one sees why Mahatma Gandhi stresses the importance of
means. It is part of his devotion to truth. Forget scruples in
the choice of means and you are likely to become dishonest.

A non-Communist who is ready to work with Communists
must face this situation: Suppose the Communists could,
with the support of camp-following non-Communists, form
a national government. This possibility has arisen in several
European countries. The Communist ministers would, in-
escapably, use their positions to dig in for a permanent stay
in office and to attack democratic institutions. That would
mean dictatorship or, if the antitotalitarians mustered the
strength, civil war. In principle, a democratic collaborator
of Communists is ready to abet dictatorship.

Moreover, Communists invariably approve of Moscow's
actions. They approved of the Soviet-Nazi pact. What do
non-Communists do then? Go along, or part company for
a few months? The Baruch Plan to outlaw the atomic bomb
was a long step toward internationalism and world government. For nationalistic reasons of its own, Moscow rejected
the Baruch Plan. The Communists said, ditto. The Soviet
government established friendly relations with Dictator
Perón of Argentina. Thereupon the Communists of Argentina began to support Perón. Identification with Russia

turns radicals and liberals into reactionaries. How then can non-Communists join hands with Communists? To do so is to put expediency above principle, power above ideas. That is the opening wedge of totalitarianism. Thus common action with totalitarians promotes totalitarianism in anti-totalitarians.

A Communist is not merely a friend of Russia. He believes in dictatorship. He believes in terror. He believes in and uses totalitarian techniques. An honest, consistent Communist would have to admit that he wanted his own country ruled by Russia (Polish, Rumanian, Hungarian, and other Communists serve as tools of Russian rule) or by a dictatorship similar to and allied to Russia. Abandoned by all who do not share this abnormal yearning, a puny, isolated Communist party, functioning legally in a country like the United States where the Communists are numerically few, would give daily proof of the sterility of its ideas and aims. But linked with non-Communist collaborationists, the Communists can, and do, split the labor and liberal movements and thereby strengthen the right conservatives. Communism is the reactionaries' greatest asset, and vice versa. The stronger the Communists the stronger the reactionaries, and the stronger the reactionaries the stronger the Communists.

On the other hand, a strong, left-of-center middle hurts both extremes. In England, for instance, eighteen months after the Labor government took office, the membership of the British Communist party, according to its own charts, had dropped from forty-three thousand to thirty-three thousand. The existence of a left-of-center government, backed by the middle and working classes, makes the British Communists a negligible quantity and makes the Tories so disconsolate that at their annual convention in Blackpool in the summer of 1946, Winston Churchill called on God to help the party.

In India, the Gandhi-Nehru-led Congress party has worked long and passionately for independence; the growing Socialist party seeks to cure social ills. The Communists, consequently, cannot pose as the sole saviors of country or class. Their popularity is proportionately diminished. Similarly, the Japanese elections of April 1947, after the worst reactionaries and militarists had been purged, brought the Socialists a great victory and the Communists a resounding defeat.

In their common dislike of the middle and their common desire to get rid of the middle, both extremes use the same weapons in the same way. "There is no middle," say the reactionaries. "Every militant democrat, Socialist, fighting trade-unionist, and New Dealer is a Communist." They try to create panic: "Reds Under Every Bed." Extremes flourish in an atmosphere of panic, tension, witch-hunting, and violence.

Likewise the Communists. They attack the reactionaries, but their greenest hate is reserved for the liberal and the Socialist who differs with them. The democrat who criticizes Communists and Russia because he is a democrat becomes a "reactionary" or a "Fascist" to the Communists. Or, worst of all, he is a "Trotskyite." By dint of repetition and with the help of a hiss and a sneer, "Trotskyite" has become the dirtiest cussword in the vocabulary of Stalinists who have no first-hand knowledge of Leon Trotsky's record or writings.

Faint hearts among the liberals who fear the mud slung by reactionaries cower and compromise and moderate their attacks on capitalist evils. Frail minds among the liberals quail under the same kind of intellectual terror exercised by Communists. This is what the extremists want.

Liberals, Socialists, progressives, radicals, and all others who work for a democratic world must never allow themselves to be silenced or terrorized by the extremes. Nor must democrats succumb to the call of one extreme to fight the other. The war for democracy is a two-front war against rightist reactionaries and against Communists. An alliance with antidemocrats cannot serve democracy.

Democrats do not have to choose between reaction and Communism. Nor between Fascism and Communism. That would be no choice at all. The choice is democracy or dictatorship, impatient evolution leading to freedom or expensive revolution leading to totalitarianism, the morality of Mahatma Gandhi or the power monopoly of Generalissimo Stalin, the inalienable right to personal liberty or the occasional opportunity to speak by the grace of the secret police, government limited to what individuals cannot do for themselves or ubiquitous government dedicated to prying, spying, and constant interference in the details of daily life, man with dignity or man a cog in the machine of state or in the equally dehumanized machine of monopolized private enterprise, man a fully active participant in fixing the conditions of his work and life or man selling his labor and time as he would a basket of onions.

These are the alternatives.

Having chalked a sharp line between themselves and the Communists and between themselves and the rightists (but Fascists and reactionaries do not normally filter into left-of-center groups), the liberal democrats and the Social Democrats can clearly state their moral and ideological goals and proceed toward them.

CHAPTER NINE

WHAT IS NEW?

THE defenders of what-is fear any change away from capitalism. They regard the introduction of the least bit of socialism as the doom of capitalism. They say the alternative is capitalism or socialism.

The Communists use the same black-and-white formulation because they want to capture those who are dissatisfied with capitalism.

In truth, however, the choice is not between Capitalism and Socialism. There is no pure capitalism. Socialism exists side by side with capitalism in every democratic country.

Socialism is the participation of government in economic affairs with a view to public welfare rather than, primarily, to private profit. The Tennessee Valley Authority (TVA) is socialism. The Grand Coulee Dam in Washington, built and operated by the United States government, is socialism. Municipal or state operation of buses, trolleys, or electric power lines is socialism. An adult mind will not fear the word.

A community instructs its government to take over an industrial enterprise when it thinks public management will be better than private management. It is usually for some such reason that governments acquire new economic functions.

During the First World War, foreign governments in need of help received loans from American banks like J. P. Morgan, the National City Bank, etc. During the Second World War, foreign governments in need of help got it from the United States government as Lend-Lease. During the First World War, expanding private munitions-makers borrowed from banks. During the Second World War, most of the industrial expansion for military purposes was a United States government operation.

Why this contrast between the conduct of the First and Second World Wars? Because the task of supplying the money and arms for war had become too big for private business.

The job now of reconstructing Europe and of constructing Asia is every bit as gigantic as that which faced America in fighting the Axis. American business, with all its fabulous wealth, could not shoulder the burden of warmaking. How can impoverished Europe and under-developed Asia solve bigger problems without government participation, that is, without socialism?

Every bomb and shell exploded during the war destroyed private capital. War work exhausted factories and machines. Inflation born of war wiped out capital savings. It is said that wars are made by capitalism. Perhaps. But the Second World War was the unmaking of capitalism.

No less important than the diminished capital resources of Europe and Asia is the diminished faith in capitalists and capitalism. Prominent capitalists in France, Italy, Germany, and Japan were hand in glove with the Nazis and Fascists. Many of them have therefore been purged by the foreign occupying powers or by their own people. They cannot resume their former positions in the community.

Man could not go through two wars in one generation and the economic turmoil, mass unemployment, and political uncertainty of the period between those two wars without beginning to entertain grave doubts about the basic ideas on which modern society rests.

It is the minor industrial producer, the retail merchant, the teacher, lawyer, doctor, dentist, government official, and small farmer—the middle class—who has, in recent decades, undergone the deepest crisis of faith. Inflation reduces their salaries and accumulated wealth. The little man is crushed or absorbed by the big trust or chain store. Insecure, its existence threatened, the middle class looks for new alliances. Politically, it is a floating island.

In a modern industrial society, the middle class is large enough to determine which way a country is to go. The German middle class succumbed to Hitler, and Germany consequently went Nazi. In Britain the middle class has sided with labor. Working-class votes alone could not have given the Labor party its overwhelming Parliamentary majority. The middle class did that. The middle class has lost faith in the former British ruling class (which, incidentally, has lost some faith in itself). The middle class, and labor, watched the decline of British industry before the war. Appreciable British capital traveled overseas rather than remaining at home to rebuild obsolete enterprises and give the country adequate housing. The British coal industry had become derelict under private direction. It was insufficiently mechanized, insufficiently financed, and woefully mismanaged. That is why it was the first to be nationalized. A government is more likely to take over where private capital has done a bad job.

The British public, moreover, saw the bankruptcy of British foreign policy; the Second World War could have been prevented by timely action, but wasn't. The British people knew, because they are politically mature, that the empire had to be liquidated or it would liquidate itself. But Churchill, wedded to the nineteenth century, had announced that he would not do it.

The Tories are the past. Britain looked to the future. Hence the Labor government. It was given a mandate to build a new England in a changing world.

On the European continent, broken persons are being asked to repair a broken world. They wield the trowel, they guide the plow, they turn the lathe, they push the pen with hands that tremble from long fatigue, undernourishment, and, worst of all, the recollection of hurtling fires, unburied corpses, and a life that is gone. These people have died. They died and they are alive again, and they wonder how it happened, and they see life with strange, bewildered, searching eyes. Human beings who were dead must eke out an existence on twelve hundred calories and not a drop of hope. A new idea may resurrect their spirit. The old is their cemetery; they were buried in it.

Europe—the mother of America and of Western culture, Europe—the home in which the religions incubated in Asia grew to maturity—Europe is badly mutilated. Unless Europe survives, civilization will be like a cripple minus a leg and arm, like a person whose sight has been dimmed. It will

require all the resources of science, progress, wealth, kindness, and freedom to bring Europe back to full life.

Asia—the lumbering giant, the sleeping colossus, the
brawn that has not yet evolved a co-ordinating brain—Asia
—more populous than all the other continents combined—
needs science to cure its physical diseases, cool its torrid
heat, water its deserts, shorten its distances, uncover its
hidden treasures, clothe its nakedness, and bring forth
enough rice and wheat and milk so that millions do not
starve to death each year.

Africa and Latin America are likewise waiting for the
magic touch.

These things are more important than system.

The purpose of human endeavor is not the maintenance
of capitalism or socialism or communism. Man's purpose
should be the greater happiness of man, and if this can be
derived under some arrangement other than pure capitalism, how could anybody object who is interested in people
and not just in a system or an ism?

Capitalism has succeeded. But capitalism has also failed.
Under its flag, continents have lain fallow, countries have
waded in their own blood, and even the richest nations have
suffered from periodic slumps, devaluation of money, unemployment, and insecurity. Some treat capitalism as
though it were a fundamentalist religion. But there is nothing unalterable, much less sacrosanct, in it.

Man is the end, not system. Freedom is the goal not
"free" enterprise—which is not free.

The Old World has no faith in the old system. Europe
and Asia are groping for something new in which they can

have confidence and that will restore their self-confidence.

Suffering nations question, doubt, and suspect. This mood could breed a dictator. But it is above all a mood conducive to experimentation and change—they have only their miseries and memories to lose. Conservatives are met with an astonished, "What, conserve that past?"

How conservative you are frequently depends on how good the past has been to you, or on how far you are from the less fortunate, or on your imagination: whether you can foresee a brighter future for humanity. The pessimistic conservatives of each era are sure nothing could be better than the present unless it be the past. The reformers are the optimists. They feel they can do better.

The three rival social philosophies that dominate the thinking of the twentieth century are: conservatism—unaltered capitalism as of 1880 or 1907; capitalism modified by socialism; communism.

Many who offer lip service to unadulterated capitalism have benefited from government aid to their own private businesses. Some of the most stalwart champions of capitalism-as-it-was were instrumental in introducing government into economic affairs. Every advocate of free enterprise avails himself of official protection.

The question is no longer whether government should be in business; it is in business. The question now is how much government there should be in business.

Most democratic countries are now grappling with the problem of the extent of government participation in economic affairs. A wise, timely solution of this problem will guarantee the survival and flowering of democracy. For the degree of official economic activity will determine how much power the state and how much power the individual is to have. And that is the core of the problem of freedom.

Some, reconciled to limited change, envisage the government in the role of regulator, arbitrator, "Santa Claus," or financier of public works such as highways and bridges. Others go further; they recommend government ownership and operation of industries. Which industries? How many? This is a subject of dispute. The nationalization of public utilities, of railroads, of coal, of heavy industries like steel —all have their advocates.

These issues will not be decided by word-juggling theorists but by the relationship of competing political and economic forces in each country. Generally speaking, at least in the remaining democracies, the decision will reflect the public's opinion of the past success or failure of capitalism.

Even in rich America, Republican Senator Robert A. Taft, not usually regarded as a socialist, declared on March 18, 1947, "Private enterprise has never provided necessary housing for the lowest-income groups." This is shown by a survey of the National Housing Agency in 1945 which reports that more than 16 per cent of the private homes in United States cities are without running water, more than two-thirds are without a private bath, almost two-thirds have no inside toilet, and almost two-thirds have dangerous or inadequate heating.

Private enterprise builds homes for profit, and where the profit is small, as it must be in houses for low-income groups, private enterprise is not much interested; the people's health and happiness suffer. Senator Taft, therefore, asserted that the providing of inexpensive shelter was the .essential responsibility of government.

With government financing, the job of housing the poor —who need housing most—might still be unattractive to private business, and perhaps, accordingly, the government would construct the homes. That would be socialism.

Greater attention to those who are depressed would tend to increase the government share in economic activity. Generally speaking, however, pressure in the United States for the scrapping of the capitalist system or for its basic alteration is weak because the system is so strong and functions to the advantage of so many. A business slump intensifies this pressure. At all times, it is greatest where groups have become aware that they are victims of economic or racial or other injustices. Sometimes it is personal:

Mrs. Clare Luce states that she was drawn to psychoanalysis and then Communism before entering the Catholic Church. "I suspect now," she writes, "that the appeal of Communism to me lay in its religious aspect. Communism was a complete authoritarian religious structure." Similarly, Heywood Broun first tried Communism and then accepted Catholicism. Louis Budenz, left the Catholic Church, became managing editor of the Communist *Daily Worker*, but is now back in his old Church. Other such persons study Stalin's sacred scriptures by the side of private swimming pools in Hollywood or plan the revolution on Connecticut estates. They wish to atone for wealth which gives them no joy but which they will not give up. So they vicariously join the poor proletariat, making sure, however, that it is comfortable and safe. The way they make a heaven out of Russia—which they do not know—reveals an inner weakness.

Psychological, philosophical, or emotional motives, or racial ties (the fact that they are Slavs working for "Mother Russia") impel some individuals toward totalitarian Communism. A highly developed moral sense or a conviction, rooted in a knowledge of history, science, and society, that capitalism is not the final form of human organization, may impel other individuals toward democratic Socialism. But neither school finds widespread support when America gives promises and prosperity.

In less favored nations, the anticapitalist compulsion is more insistent.

With few exceptions, the democratic nations of Europe and Asia, and some in Latin America, are moving fast toward state participation in economics. Sweden, England, France, Italy, Australia, New Zealand, Austria, and western Germany have nationalized big industries. Where governments have not taken over industries they are either preparing to do so or instituting rigid controls or otherwise bringing private business under state supervision. Private capitalism, a weaker reed since the war, leans increasingly on government. And governments, reflecting popular distrust, are keeping a closer watch and tighter grip on private enterprise.

Capitalism is losing political support in democratic countries. The Conservative party of Great Britain announced on May 11, 1947, that if it were returned to office it would not attempt to restore the Bank of England, the coal mines, or the railroads to private ownership. In France, the Communist and Socialist parties are anticapitalist, and the Catholic party has a strong anticapitalist wing. Those are the three biggest parties of the country. Even General Charles de Gaulle, far right in France, declared publicly on April 24, 1947, that he favored the nationalization of the coal industry, electricity, and insurance. In Italy, a similar situation exists. The German Christian Social Union, which includes Catholics and Protestants, favors nationalization of some industries. Only one small German party is for pure capitalism. The Chinese nationalist government operates a giant textile manufacturing syndicate which competes with private producers. The Socialist party of Japan appeals to a large part of the electorate. Mr. A. K. Gani, Minister of Economics in the new Indonesian republic—population fifty-five million—has announced a ten-year plan to convert Java and Sumatra to "semi-Socialism." The new central government of India has decided to nationalize the Reserve Bank of India and is building ten thousand houses for coal miners in Bengal and Bihar. India's growing Socialist party is led by Jayaprakash Narayan, who is regarded by Jawarhlal Nehru, big capitalists like J. R. D. Tata, and others as the coming leader of his country. India's Socialists—because they are a purely non-religious party—may be best equipped to deal with the rivalry between Hindus and Moslems. The most numerous Jewish group in Palestine is the Jewish Labor Party. Sizeable Socialist organizations have long existed throughout Europe. The most important of these is the British Labor party.

Capitalism is losing its intellectuals. The creative intellectual forces of democratic Europe and Asia are either religious, Socialist, or Communist. Only a stray thinker or analyst enters the lists on the two continents to break a lance for private enterprise.

Throughout the Soviet sphere of influence in Europe—in Finland, Poland, Russian Germany, Russian Austria, Rumania, Hungary, Czechoslovakia, Bulgaria, Yugoslavia, and Albania—the bulk of the economy has been nationalized under Russian and Communist pressure. Moscow trusts and cartels control decisive percentages of the production and trade of this vast area.

The social spectrum thus shades from capitalistic America with very little socialism, to the democratic parts of Europe and Asia where socialism is rapidly being mixed with capitalism, to the Soviet sphere of influence where there is less democracy and more socialism each month, to the undemocratic Soviet Union where private capitalism is nonexistent.

This is the new postwar world picture. Everywhere, the war has accelerated the trend away from capitalism.

CHAPTER TEN

HOW TO ADJUST TO
MODERN CONDITIONS

MANKIND is witnessing an insane drive for power. Major nation gobbles minor nation; giant company absorbs pygmy company; trade-unions hold a club over industry and government. Each side justifies its actions by pointing to the equal, and opposite, actions of its rivals. Each is at least partly right.

The fantastic expansion of production in modern times is the root of the power problem. The richer an economy the greater the power possessed by the economic and political groups who own or direct it. Clearly, the total economic and political power in the United States, for instance, is vastly bigger today than in 1890 simply because there is more output, more buying, more money, more everything.

Gandhi would deal with this situation by keeping life simple and primitive with many cottage industries in self-governing villages. But even India does not follow him in this matter and the world certainly will not.

Can constructive techniques be devised in our complicated industrial civilization for curbing power or for reducing the total amount of power? Unless such devices are found, scientific discoveries and technological inventions, which ought to be blessings, will become the means of enslaving or exterminating mankind.

Some argue that if power and capital are to be monopolized they would be safer in the keeping of a government that is the agent of the public than in private hands. They accordingly advocate a transfer of all power from capitalists to governments. But that neither eliminates nor reduces the menace to freedom, for whereas capitalists in a democracy can be regulated by the state and checked by unions, a government which owns all capital is the unassailable autocrat.

The more a government does the more power it gets; the more power it gets the more power it has over the individual. In Russia the state does everything. It is the sole capitalist and administrator. From this, flow exploitation, oppression, dictatorship, and imperialism. Marxists used to assume that the mere transfer of the private capitalists' assets to the state would introduce the millennium. But a state owning all real estate becomes a monster in size and cruelty—and what then has man gained?

The alternative to dictatorship is obviously not Gandhi's spinning-wheel economy. Nor is it an arrangement in which the government does nothing in economic matters. That would result in chaos and insecurity.

The evil is the monopoly of power by either the government or the private capitalist. Both tend to make a robot of man. Monopolized power is undemocratic.

The cure is the diffusion or more equal distribution of power.

Like so many countries in recent years, Australia has seen small companies swallowed by bigger ones; the tendency is toward fewer and larger corporations. Accordingly, Labor in Australia urged the government to go into business. "In my opinion," said the Australian Prime Minister, a Laborite, "there is room here for both."

Private industry under the free enterprise system is sometimes so highly concentrated in a few trusts that competition is stifled. When the government and private capital are both in industry there can be competition.

The British government's present nationalization program includes the coal industry, rail and road transportation, gas, electricity, and cable and wireless communications; public utilities, in fact. These employ approximately 10 per cent of the working population. The remaining 90 per cent will still be privately employed.

This is mixed economy. It may become the new pattern in many democracies. Mixed economy is a combination of private capitalism and government capitalism.

The atomic bomb was developed by an intimate partnership between the United States government and private industry. The experiments looking to the use of atomic energy for civilian purposes are likewise being conducted by the federal government with help from business corporations. Atomic energy is so close to military affairs and so crucial in world politics that the government must play an important part in its control. At some future date, therefore, the government may be the chief, indeed the only, source of atomic energy for industry. Atomic energy might change the entire face of production—by eliminating coal mining, for instance.

The government, manufacturing atomic energy social-istically, would supply it to private capitalistic factories. That would be mixed economy. Modern science made cap-italism what it is. More modern science may completely alter capitalism.

In a mixed economy, ownership and operation of the means of production are not divided only between the federal government and private corporations. Ownership and operation are divided among the federal government, state or provincial governments, county governments, city governments, co-operatives, private companies, and private individuals.

Such wide distribution of economic power would prevent political dictatorship and encourage initiative and activity in large numbers; in other words, it would establish eco-nomic democracy fortified by political democracy.

One of the greatest advantages of mixed economy would be over-all, voluntary planning by private business in con-junction with the government. A family plans, a school plans, a factory owner plans. There is need, however, of a plan among businesses. Formerly, social scientists believed the relations between various branches of an economy did not need regulation or planning; they regulated themselves automatically through prices and through supply and de-mand. But one has only to look at the dislocation, the bank-ruptcies, and the strikes caused by high prices and under-consumption to realize that automatic regulation is often too costly, and frequently does not regulate.

If private enterprises tried to plan on a national scale they might fall out, or they might be accused of organizing a monopoly in restraint of trade.

Governments are regulating now. They endeavor to keep prices down, to distribute income by taxation, to adjust wages, to increase employment, etc. But usually this is done haphazardly after troubles have appeared. The troubles ought to be anticipated and, at least in part, forestalled.

That would be the function of mixed-economy planning.

Planning would mean less bureaucratic regulation and more automatic gearing of the innumerable parts of a nation's business life.

At present, capitalism is working too chaotically and anarchistically by the unscientific method of blind trial and grievous error. We know much more about next week's weather than about next week's markets. Even politics is more co-ordinated than business.

Mixed economy would add not only order, it would also add a new incentive. It would increase the efforts of working people. In times of high or full employment, when workers are sure of their jobs, they may be inclined to slacken their efforts. It is possible that the world is entering a period of high employment. Labor shortages exist on the European continent and in Great Britain.

The Black Death plague which smote England in 1348-9 wiped out between a third and a half of the population of the island. The consequent scarcity of labor enabled the serfs to leave the land and move to the towns where they made possible the development of industry and of British capitalism.

In like manner, the present labor scarcity in Great Britain necessitates more mechanization and rationalization than private enterprise has, to date, been ready to undertake. Thus the shortage of manpower is one of the forces driving toward Socialism in England. Provided personal freedom is guaranteed and bureaucracy does not grow too lush, a state enterprise may, in time of high employment, be more productive than a private business because the worker may have a sense of working for himself, for the community.

Mixed economy, finally, would be conducive to economic democracy.

In a political democracy, the executive, the legislative, and the judiciary branches check and balance each other. This triangle is a guarantee of liberty. A system of checks and balances is also needed in economic affairs. The present economic triangle is government regulation of capitalists and trade-unions, and trade-union opposition to capitalists. It has its virtues. But the economic checks and balances would probably work more automatically and smoothly if production and distribution were shared between the government, private capitalists, and groups of individuals organized in co-operatives.

This mixed-economy method of breaking up monopoly and introducing more competition is one method of coping with the power problem. It is not enough. Another way ought to be tried: the curtailing of the total amount of power available to anybody. Many possibilities exist:

In India, the loan shark lends a poor peasant a huge sum at an exorbitant rate of interest. Thereafter, often unto death, the peasant is the usurer's economic serf. A land bank or a mutual-aid loan society would abolish the power of the lender over the borrower.

By discarding the use of passports and visas between friendly countries, consular bureaucrats would be deprived of their power to delay, obstruct, and irritate travelers.

Lynchings do not merely kill one or six or ten Negroes a year. They intimidate millions of Negroes and thereby make a mockery of their paper freedom. A regime of law would rob white barbarians of their power over Negroes.

Planned parenthood enables mothers and fathers to dispose freely of their lives.

A businessman who owns the one or two newspapers and the radio station of a town can, merely because he inherited the money or sold shoes successfully, acquire a hold on the minds of thousands. Competition is needed. Where competition is impossible, the owner should be conscious of a special social responsibility to present all sides of questions fairly.

It is much more important for every family to own its own home than to own an automobile. If every family owned its home or its apartment in an urban co-operative apartment house, the power of the landlords for evil would shrink. Toward the same end, cities might do well to own the land on which they are built.

A civilized procedure is needed for the fixing of wages, working conditions, and prices in the telegraph, telephone, transportation, and other monopoly or near-monopoly industries—which are really public utilities—to prevent a trade union from paralyzing the life of a nation. That would reduce the total power available.

Farm land should be as free as air. It should not be bought or sold. It should be parceled out by the community to families and individuals in accordance with their capacity to use the land and with a view to the public welfare. The acreage held by any one person should be strictly limited. In this way, nonproducing landlords would lose their power over the men, women, and children who produce the world's food and industrial crops.

A high level of employment with adequate social-security and unemployment insurance puts salary and wage earners in a better position to bargain for working conditions. They consequently acquire greater independence in relation to employers.

Political party machines that can directly or indirectly nominate candidates for office have too much power; they hamper democracy. More political activity by rank-and-file voters curbs the machines.

Poll taxes or property tests for voters or candidates concentrate too much power in too few hands. Those limitations on democracy can be rescinded by an aroused public.

A mining company that owns the homes and stores in a mining village has too much power over the men it employs. This can be remedied.

When education is an expensive privilege, the few who can afford it enjoy a tremendous advantage over those who cannot. Free public education for all reduces this power advantage.

Similarly, equality of wealth would eradicate the p

advantage now inherent in wealth. Equality of wealth is unattainable for a long time. But a gradual approach to equality between individuals would begin to solve the problem of power.

Even if wealth were equalized, power could not be. There will always be officials and laymen, top officials and low officials. How each behaves will depend in part on adequate laws and checks and balances. But corruption and abuse of power will still be possible, and in the final analysis, therefore, everything comes down to the moral quality of the individual and the public.

A person desirous of being a bullying master seeks an outlet for his indecent urge and can find it in a family, a schoolroom, an office, a factory, a government job. He needs a cure, preferably one administered by himself after looking into a mirror and into the lives of those he torments. Similarly, if tradition and custom condone bribes, spoils, nepotism, favoritism at the inevitable cost of efficiency, and other forms of public immorality, then the community suffers no matter what statutes have been voted.

Economic, bureaucratic, and legalistic ways of combatting social ills have to be supplemented by the individual operating on his character and the community setting higher ethical standards.

System counts. A Gandhi would not get very far in a dictatorship. Dictatorship tries, and usually succeeds in expunging individual deviations toward goodness. The terror of a dictatorship makes everybody conform to a norm of evil.

In democracy, on the other hand, each person has a

wide margin in which either his virtue or its lack plays an enormous role.

It used to be thought that improved morality would result automatically when private capitalism ended. Soviet experience is one argument against this thesis. Soviet society is impressively immoral. "Morality?" says a character in *Unknown Artist*, a Soviet novel by V. Kaverin published in 1931, "I have no time to think of the word. I am busy. I am building socialism. But if I had to choose between morality and a pair of trousers, I would choose the trousers." He would choose the trousers not merely because trousers are in short supply but because morality is low-priced. How can it be high-priced where the lie is an official weapon, and where terror puts a premium on safety-at-any-price?

Soviet experience is not conclusive. But it is a warning— especially when one observes the acts of non-Russian Communists who are no less unscrupulous than their Muscovite trainers. Karl Marx (Socialism) enslaved by Peter the Great (Russian nationalism) becomes a perversion. Marx with Gandhi might make a fruitful combination. Economic reforms and revolutions are not enough. Dictators flourish on the cheapness of life, on indifference to human suffering, on dishonesty. Combat these and you combat dictatorship. Children and adults in democracies would be less accessible to the immoral ideas of totalitarianism if democratic life taught them the value of life, freedom, and truth; if they learned to practice human kindness, humility, and friendship. No amount of socialization will teach men to love flowers or a sunset or to be kind to animals. Equally, nothing in the nature of government or economics can quickly inculcate a love of mankind.

Ultimately, the nature of government and of the economic system depends on the character of the men in them and on how watchful the people are. Plato said it twenty-three hundred years ago when he declared that "the human race would never see the end of trouble until true lovers of wisdom should come to hold political power, or the holders of political power should, by some divine appointment, become true lovers of wisdom."

The rescue of democracy from the dangers besetting it is, above all, a moral undertaking which must start in each individual. Peace and democracy, like charity, begin at home, in the hearts of men.

As with government and economic associations, so with religions and churches; they are as moral as the people in them. Mahatma Gandhi, who is supremely religious, whose morality, philosophy, and mode of living spring in fact entirely from his religion, says, "I have noticed no definite progress in any religion. The world would not be the shambles it has become if the religions of the world were progressive." The head of the Greek Orthodox Church in Russia proclaims Stalin "the anointed of God." Germans of all denominations forgot their Christianity when, as passionate nationalists, they supported Hitler. Catholic churchmen and laymen helped and help Dictator Franco, although, according to Francis C. McMahon, leading Catholic layman writing in the New York *Post* of April 30, 1947, the Catholic Church in Spain "is permitted only such latitude as fosters the interests of the dictator." The Catholic clergy of Italy actively aided Mussolini's rape of Ethiopia; bishops collected gold for it.

Religions are too ready to compromise with the powers-that-be instead of militantly fighting the evil of power.

Christ was moral and democratic. How many Christians follow Christ? The caste system in Hinduism is immoral and undemocratic. How many Hindus follow Gandhi in fighting against it? Islam teaches brotherhood; it is a very democratic religion. How democratic is Egypt, Iraq, Transjordan, Iran, or Saudia Arabia? Judaism has a code of high ethics. How many Jews follow it?

Churches are moral when they grapple in a concrete way with the problem of too much power and monopolized power.

CHAPTER ELEVEN

WHAT ARE THE REASONS FOR
RUSSIA'S POWER IN THE WORLD?

THE world's biggest power problem is Russia. Stalin is the most powerful individual on earth. He is a man of power and knows the laws of power. He consciously acquired vast power at home and now he has acquired vast power abroad.

How is it that the Soviet Union can compete with America and indeed, with the entire democratic world? The Soviet government has given its people neither adequate groceries nor sufficient liberties. Russia is militarily weaker than America. Freedom is obviously better than dictatorship. How can Communists nevertheless compete with democratic parties?

What is the source of Russian power and Communist influence throughout the world?

During the recent Paris Peace Conference an old Paris barber had just finished cutting my hair. Foolishly, I asked for an olive-oil shampoo.

"Olive oil!" he gasped. "On your hair! We can't get it for our stomachs." He complained about conditions. "Next time I'm voting Communist," he declared. "Everybody else has tried and failed. I'm for giving the Communists a chance. They say they can do it."

The barber was no Communist, but conditions were bad. He had lost faith in capitalism. He did not have much to lose. I talked about liberty. "Bah, liberty," he exclaimed. "I will always find work. I managed under the Nazis too." That explains one vote for the French Communist party. He was not the only one.

I was in Jerusalem in the summer of 1942. Nazi Marshal Rommel was reaching out for the Suez Canal and Cairo. Had he succeeded, the war would have turned against the anti-Axis coalition. Arab leaders in Jerusalem told me that the Arabs of Palestine were hoping for Rommel's advance and preparing to welcome him. Why? The Arabs were anti-British; the Nazis were fighting the British; therefore the Arabs were pro-Nazi.

In the summer of 1946 I was again in Jerusalem. A noted Arab lady asked me to dinner in her home near the slope of Mt. Scopus. Several young Arab leaders were present. One Arab said, "If the British impose a pro-Zionist solution here the Arabs will turn to Russia." Another Arab remarked, "Seeking salvation from Russia is like catching hold of a shark to save yourself from drowning." Nevertheless, not a few Arabs flirt with Moscow. The formula is the same: the Arabs feel anti-British; Russia wants the British out of the Near East; therefore some Arabs are pro-Russian.

If things are black you want a change even though you are not quite sure just what the change will bring. Dissatisfied people or suffering people think of happiness in terms of the reverse of their present circumstances.

Propaganda in favor of Communism often falls on ground fertilized by prolonged privations and oppression. The Russian system is offered as ideal because it has abolished the large landlord and the private capitalist and substituted economic planning with state ownership. The hungry sharecropper in China is fascinated by this tale of a land that has expelled the gouging rent collector and speculator; he does not inquire into the Soviet standard of living and is little interested in freedom of the press.

Russia, moreover, is portrayed to Asiatics and Africans as the champion of enslaved colonies. To be sure, Russia herself enslaves foreign nations. She looted Manchuria. She reverted to czarist policy in taking Port Arthur as a naval base and Dairen as a port under her partial control. She reverted to czarist policy in extorting an oil concession from the Iranian government while the Red Army was on Iranian soil. She reverted to czarist policy when she asked for joint defense of the Dardanelles.

But these facts are new and the propagandists omit them. Emphasis is on Vishinsky's debate with British Foreign Secretary Ernest Bevin in which the Russian appeared as the friend of Indonesia. Emphasis is on Foreign Minister Molotov's vote for India's United Nations' resolution against Jim Crow ghettoes in South Africa.

The teeming millions of the Orient see the situation in its simplest and crudest terms: they want freedom from foreign imperialists. The foreign imperialists are Great Britain, France, Holland, and Portugal. America sides with England. Russia opposes the imperialists. Therefore the colonials regard Russia with a friendly eye.

The observer in Asia finds a rising tide of antiwhite and anti-West sentiment. Such zenophobia is ugly and uncivilized. It is part of the descent of modern man into the abyss from which salvation will be difficult. It is akin to the racial hate of the Nazis and the color prejudice of the "white-supremacy" barbarians of the United States. It does violence to Gandhi's teachings. It is one of the most dangerous symptoms of these dangerous times.

In India, I talked with Chakravarti Rajagopalacharia, member of the Indian government, old friend of Gandhi, one of the veteran leaders of the Indian nationalist movement. He said, "America had the atomic bomb while fighting Germany. But she did not drop the bomb on the Germans because they are white. She dropped it on the Japanese because they are colored." Nothing could dissuade him. I heard the same statement many times in Asia. It is not true. The United States did not have the atomic bomb before Hitler's defeat. Rajagopalacharia's assertion was not based on proof. But it was based on the knowledge that the white man discriminates against colored people.

Of the two billion persons on this earth, about one billion three hundred million are colored: four hundred and fifty million in China; four hundred million in India; Japan, Indo-China, Indonesia, Malay, Burma, Africa, etc. No one interest connects them; but anticolor persecution anywhere is likely to irk them all.

Lynchings (one of the first questions Gandhi put to me was, "How many lynchings has America had this year?") and anti-Negro bigotry in the United States, restrictions on Indians in South Africa, and white imperialism generally turn them against the West. They then look for leadership elsewhere. Communists have played important roles in the liberation movements of Burma, Indo-China, and Indonesia.

The colonies of the East strive for liberation from imperialists who are capitalistic; that makes them receptive to anticapitalist guidance and education. The colonial can only think of foreign businessmen as his exploiters.

It all helps the Communists. "The opponents of the Reds," writes the conservative New York *Herald Tribune*, "would have much less to worry about, especially in Asia, if they did their best to remedy the evils of which Communists take advantage."

Asia wants food and independence. Europe, troubled and torn, insecure and poor, likewise searches for the secret of renewal and survival. Russia is ready with the answer.

Colonel Tulpanov, the chief Soviet contact man with foreigners in Germany, said to a German political leader, "You, and all Germans, must choose between America and Russia. America is rich and has much to give. But an economic slump is coming in the United States and it will pull you down if you tie yourself to America just as the collapse after the Wall Street crash in 1929 affected many European nations adversely. Russia is not as rich as America. But our economy is stable."

The German leader was not convinced. He was not sure that Russian economy was stable or that an American business depression impended. He had had enough of dictatorship. The Russians, however, will try again. They know that Europe craves stability.

The Communists also point out that Russia is in Europe

to stay; America may withdraw. Accordingly, some Europeans hesitate to commit themselves by openly revealing their sympathies for America; they realize it would go hard with them if the Americans retired.

What a Russian says in Germany is echoed in a dozen places around the globe. Among others, the daily *Ta Kung Pao* of Tientsin, China, predicted on April 3, 1947, according to a dispatch by Benjamin Welles in *The New York Times*, that "in ten years the United States will suffer a far greater depression than that in 1929. If this occurs, the newspaper expects the United States might leave the United Nations, give up the Middle East and evacuate Asia." The same article in the Chinese paper criticized American imperialism.

This fits perfectly into the Soviet scheme of confusing and disturbing the world about America's future. Meanwhile, Russia pushes on.

Russia's proximity to Europe and Asia and her aggressiveness are part of her strength. Moscow, for instance, asked Turkey to cede two of her provinces to Russia and to allow the Bolshevik regime to share in the defense of the Dardanelles—which would be tantamount to the subjugation of Turkey. Russia made no move however; she merely made demands; she threw her large shadow across Turkey. Alarmed, the Turks mobilized a huge portion of their manpower and maintained their army in fighting condition at such tremendous expense that their national economy began to crack. (Hitler did something similar with Austria, Czechoslovakia, and France. He hollowed out their hearts with a war of nerves before marching his troops in.)

Gloating over this cheap success, the Communists went to work with propaganda. "Turkey is undemocratic," they shouted. "Turks massacred Armenians. The Turks did not enter the Second World War until it was almost over." These statements are all true, and so naive folks shook their heads sadly and agreed that Turkey does not deserve help—which was exactly the result the Communists wanted.

From the creation of the new Turkey by Kemal Pasha (Atatürk) in 1919 until recently, Turkey was a one-party regime. Today, a second party is permitted restrained opposition. During Turkey's long one-party life, Soviet Russia's relations with Turkey were extremely friendly. Russian help saved Turkey from Greece and England in the Anatolian war of 1921 and 1922. Thereafter, Moscow gave economic advice and financial aid to the Turks. At international conferences (Lausanne in 1923, for example), Russia championed Turkey's interests, the interests of one-party Turkey in which Communist activity was illegal and Communists cruelly persecuted. But now the Kremlin suddenly discovered that Turkey was not democratic.

What had changed? Russia had changed. Russia was insisting on Turkey's acceptance of her demands. The Turks resisted. Russia immediately discovered that Turkey was undemocratic. Communists immediately discovered that the Armenians of Turkey should be transferred to Russia.

On March 24, 1947, the State Department in Washington published one of the secret Big Three agreements negotiated at the Teheran conference in December 1943. According to its text, Roosevelt, Churchill, and Stalin decided "it was most desirable that Turkey should come into the war

on the side of the Allies before the end of the year." They
wanted this undemocratic Turkey on their side. And they
"took note of Marshal Stalin's statement that if Turkey
found herself at war with Germany, and as a result Bulgaria
declared war on Turkey or attacked her, the Soviet would
immediately be at war with Bulgaria." Stalin would save
undemocratic Turkey.

Turkey did not join the war at that time. She joined
much later. The Russians and Communists held this against
Turkey. But Bulgaria never joined the Allies. In fact, Bulgaria fought long as an ally of Hitler, and Russia had to
declare war on Bulgaria and invade her. Nevertheless,
Russia urged the Paris Peace Conference in 1946 to author-
ize Bulgaria, the ex-enemy, to annex territory of Greece
which staunchly resisted Italian and German attacks.

Why? Because Bulgaria is a Russian puppet and Turkey
refuses to become one.

This is one clear example of the immorality of Russian
diplomacy and the Communist strategy which confront the
democracies. Russia's nationalistic purposes come first. Moscow's policy toward a country has nothing to do with the
political character of that country. Stalin had a pact with
Hitler and with the Japanese aggressors; he made a treaty
of amity with Dictator Perón of Argentina. Russia's ideol-
ogy and politics serve to mislead others and to create illu-
sions. It ought to be completely transparent. But it isn't.

Stalin's unscrupulousness and Communist unscrupulousness have helped Russia with numerous victories.

The Soviet government is not planning to conquer the
world or even a continent by the force of its arms. That

would be difficult and foolish. The Communists are confident that with some help from Moscow in intensifying the chaos and exploiting the despair, the democracies will themselves ruin the non-Soviet world. The democracies have already made a rather large contribution toward this end.

As a result of the Stalin-Hitler pact, Russia annexed half of Poland up to the Curzon line, Esthonia, Latvia, Lithuania, and part of Rumania. As a result of the attack on Finland, Russia annexed part of Finland. As a result of Russia's military power and Stalin's dynamic diplomacy, but also thanks to Western political blunders, Russia has annexed German territory, Polish territory, Czechoslovak territory, and Japanese territory. Altogether about two hundred thousand square miles inhabited by twenty-five million people.

All these Soviet annexations violate the Atlantic Charter. Most of them violate treaties which Moscow had signed with the countries involved. The German and Czechoslovak areas and the richest slice of the Polish area (east Galicia) never belonged to Russia. The bulk of what had belonged to Russia was seized by the czars. In his pamphlet, *War and Revolution*, published in Petrograd in May 1917, Lenin condemned the partition of Courland, a part of Latvia, and Poland by Russia, Germany, and Austria-Hungary. "Courland and Poland," he wrote, "were partitioned together by the three crowned brigands. They partitioned them for a hundred years. They tore their living flesh. And the Russian brigand tore away most because he was then the strongest." Lenin regarded these land-grabs as criminal. He handed them back at the beginning of the revolution.

He stated publicly that the Bolsheviks did not wish to keep the loot of the autocrats of old Russia. Now Stalin, the autocrat of the new Russia, has grabbed them again.

If nations started taking what once belonged to them, England would take part of France, Sweden would take Leningrad, Turkey would take most of the Soviet Ukraine, Britain would take New York, the Dutch would take New York, France would take Louisiana, Spain would take California, Germany would take Alsace and Lorraine, and the world would be an even worse insane asylum than it already is. The annexations were brutal and illegal in the first place.

And what does "belong" mean? Did Poland "belong" to Russia? Did Czechoslovakia "belong" to Hitler? Did India ever "belong" to England, or was it held unjustly by force? The fact that decent people can use the word "belong" is one of the marks of our moral degradation. It was in this way that a landlord once spoke of his serfs; they were his "souls" and "belonged" to him. Now we have risen a step higher (or fallen a step lower): entire peoples "belong" to those who have the power to coerce them.

In addition to territories annexed outright, the Soviet government, after the war, occupied large parts of Korea, Germany, and Austria by agreement with the United States and Great Britain, and exercised effective control over the rumps of Finland, Poland, and Rumania, and over Czechoslovakia, Hungary, Bulgaria, Yugoslavia, Albania, and sections of Manchuria. These countries, with an approximate population of one hundred and fifty million people, constitute the Soviet sphere of influence, the new Soviet empire.

Soviet imperialism is not the effect of anti-Sovietism in the democracies or of American possession of the atomic bomb. Most of the Soviet empire was acquired while relations between Russia, England, and America were good, while Russia was receiving billions in Lend-Lease from the Western powers and before the first atomic bomb exploded. Most of the Soviet empire was acquired thanks to the complacent acquiescence of the United States and the United Kingdom.

The Soviet empire is the product of force. It exists because Germany, Italy, and Japan have collapsed, because England and France were weakened by the war, and because America was either unable or unwilling to do anything about it.

Soviet imperialism is the by-product of Russian and Ukrainian nationalism and of Soviet desire to rehabilitate war-wounded Russia with the cheap assistance of satellite nations.

There is a disturbing parallel here between the expansion of Hitler and of Stalin. Each was aided by democracies whom it most threatened. Each taught the dictator's contempt for the democracies. Viewed from Berlin and Moscow the democracies seemed to be driven by a suicidal urge. Hitler and the Japanese made the mistake of thinking they could go as far as they liked.

Imperialism has its own momentum. That is why all imperialism and expansion are bad—Russian, British, and American. Imperialism is never sated. It breeds imperialism in others and then they all argue like school children about who started it.

Hitler won power outside Germany by arms, by spies, by a relatively small number of Germans abroad who were more loyal to the Nazis than to their own countries, by appeasing democrats, by the collaboration of certain reactionaries, and by virtue of economic, political, and moral disintegration within the democracies.

The Second World War increased this disintegration and made it easy for Stalin to win power outside Russia. It has been so easy that he is encouraged to go on, trusting in further blunders by his competitors.

The peril of power was recognized by the framers of the Atlantic Charter. All anti-Axis belligerents signed the charter and thereby pledged themselves to "seek no aggrandizement, territorial or others . . . ." The world's experience shows that aggrandizement leads to war. England and America fought two world wars for one chief reason: to prevent a single nation from dominating Europe. Hitler as master of Europe, leagued with the Japanese masters of Asia, would have constituted a mortal peril to America and Britain. The Western powers went to war to prevent this from happening. If Russia threatened to dominate Europe, and therefore Asia, a third war would be measurably nearer.

President Truman said in Mexico City, "We have fought two world wars in one generation. We've found that the victor loses in total war as well as the vanquished." Stalin has found this too; he sees it in the devastation of Russia and in the many millions of Soviet dead (fifteen million, is the estimate) and crippled resulting from the Second

World War. The third will be worse, whoever wins or
loses. I do not believe Stalin wants a world war. I do not
believe he is planning a world war or a violent world revolution. No man says, "I will conquer the universe with my
arms and bombs." But Stalin, always eager for more power,
does take advantage of opportunities to extend it, and at
times he creates such opportunities. If they bring poverty,
anguish, and civil strife in other nations it does not matter
to him. He has said that Communist economy is the best.
He is certain that capitalism must perish, that his system
will rule the earth, and that he is the Marx-sent agent of
this transformation. He regards all of today's events as
steppingstones to Communist victory. Soviet policy and the
acts of foreign Communists indicate that Moscow sees the
present era of exhaustion, disillusionment, hopelessness, and
shortage of goods as the best chance to undermine the
democratic world, especially—as the Soviet press never
tires of asserting—since a capitalist depression is in the
offing.

Stalin expects to achieve very big things with limited
means. His greatest inspiration is the folly of his enemy
who does not understand him. Stalin hopes to obtain more
power through the decay and abdication of democracy.
That may be Russia's most fatal error.

An aggressor who has been appeased is dangerous. He
does not know when and where to stop. Since the end of
the war, Stalin has continued his forward push. He set up
a puppet government in the province of Azerbaijan in Iran
and, while Russian troops were on Iranian soil, he forced
the Teheran authorities to grant Russia an oil concession.

Months later the Azerbaijan satellite collapsed because the Iranian government, encouraged by the United States, sent its army into the province. The population welcomed the soldiers and the Russian quislings fled to the Soviet Union. This is the only setback Soviet expansionism has suffered. At Potsdam, in July 1945, Stalin told Truman and Attlee he wanted to share in the defense of the Dardanelles. Subsequently, the Soviets officially asked Turkey for this concession. It would have given Russia control over Turkey. The demand still stands. Soviet official newspapers have stated that the two Turkish provinces of Kars and Ardahan should be ceded to Russia. Tito, the Little Stalin, who looks like Goering with his medals, has officially claimed Greek Macedonia, Italian territory and parts of Austria for Yugoslavia. He continues to tug at Trieste.

Throughout the Soviet sphere of influence, Communist control becomes firmer every week. Thanks to the presence of the Red Army, the Hungarian Communists, although defeated in free elections, began taking over the government of Hungary. In Austria, the Russians seized all business enterprises which the Nazis had seized from Austrians. A large part of Austria has thus become an economic colony of Russia. Huge Soviet trusts own and operate the industries of the Russian zone in Germany which have been integrated with the economy of the Soviet Union. In spite of the calls for German unity, Moscow has actually split Germany in two and converted military occupation into permanent possession. Soviet imperialism is on the march.

It used to be said that imperialism was based on export

capital: an industrialized country had surplus capital and goods which it wanted to export. It therefore seized areas that were economically and culturally backward and turned them into colonies. But since the war, Russia has acted in reverse: she has spread into countries which are highly industrialized and, in several cases, economically and culturally superior to the Soviet Union. Through various devices and agreements, the Bolsheviks are importing the output of their new sphere of influence in order to feed their own famished home market. Soviet imperialism is based on import capital. It is the product not of surpluses but of deficits. Its effect is to exploit and impoverish the countries within its sphere.

Outside its own empire, the Soviet Union enjoys the eager collaboration of the Communist parties, whether they are in government or in opposition. Communists and pro-Communists and the naive and blind who follow them have organized the World Federation of Trade Unions (WFTU). Foreign Minister Molotov and Soviet delegate Gromyko have tried to obtain a special status for the federation in the United Nations. In several countries, notably France, the WFTU exercises tremendous political influence.

The Soviet-Slav-Communist bloc still pursues an expansionist policy. This could lead to war just as German, Italian, and Japanese expansion led to war.

The first reason for wishing to block Soviet territorial and political expansion is to prevent the third world war. If Russia gets too far other nations may grow alarmed, as England grew alarmed in 1939, and decide to fight.

In the wake of Russian power moves the glacier of dictatorship annihilating freedom as it advances. That is the second reason for opposing Soviet expansion.

During the summer of 1946, reports appeared in German newspapers about Soviet kidnappings of German boys. The Russians and Communists indignantly denied these reports. But in Berlin, that autumn, I obtained the photostat of a letter that confirmed them. The letter was written and signed by Otto Buchwitz, the head of the Communist-dominated Socialist Unity party in Russian-occupied Saxony, and was addressed to Otto Grotewohl, the head of that same party in Berlin. The letter, dated May 7, 1946, begins,

Dear Otto,

I have talked to you one or two times about the following matter. But, forced by circumstances, I must return to it again.

I have in my portfolio approximately forty cases of persons who have been arrested by the NKVD (the Soviet Secret Police. L.F.). Most of them are young people fifteen to eighteen years of age who were arrested last year.

The letter then proceeds to name two cases of adults arrested by the Russians. Neither was ever a Nazi, Buchwitz declares.

I took the photostat of this letter to the office of the Socialist Unity party in the Russian sector of Berlin and showed it to Otto Grotewohl to whom the original had been sent. He said, thanks to his intervention, several of the boys had been released.

"But I am told," I answered, "by persons, German and non-German, who have collected the names of the victims, that thousands have been arrested."

Grotewohl made no reply.

The British-licensed, Berlin daily *Telegraf* of April 6, 1947, contains an open letter by Mrs. Annedore Leber, a well-known German Social Democrat, which states, "Desperate mothers come to us because their sixteen-year-old boys have been arrested. Despite the youth amnesty, some mothers have been pining in uncertainty about their children for almost two years."

These boys are simply taken off the streets and streetcars without explanation by the Russian police who remove them to nobody knows where. In like manner, trainloads of German workingmen and scientists have been forcibly deported, after the end of the war, into Russia.

A dictatorship cannot help being true to itself. It exports the methods and morality which it employs at home.

Communists, as well as Socialists, and Christian Democrats, have their political parties in the three western zones of Germany. But in the Russian zone the Socialists, or Social Democrats, are barred; the bourgeois parties are legal but they can not put up candidates in all districts; the camouflage Communist party, called the Socialist Unity party, receive valuable material aid from the Russians.

Because Berlin is unified under an administration which is directly supervised by the four occupying foreign governments, all political parties function in all parts of the city. But whereas the Socialist Unity party covered the walls of the American, British, and French sectors of the city with their stickers and posters in the 1946 elections, the Social Democrats were not permitted to display a number of their posters in the Russian sector. Two of these

proscribed posters read: WHERE THERE IS FEAR, THERE
IS NO FREEDOM. WITHOUT FREEDOM THERE IS NO SO-
CIALISM, and NO SOCIALISM WITHOUT CIVIL LIBERTIES.
The Russians probably regarded these simple truths as
criticisms of the Soviet regime and Communism.

If the Russians can commit atrocities and exert political
pressures in Germany which, in theory at least, is ruled by
Americans, Englishmen, Frenchmen, and Russians sitting
regularly in the Allied Control Council in Berlin, it is not
difficult to imagine what goes on in countries like Hungary,
Rumania, Bulgaria, and Yugoslavia where Communists
and Russians dominate and where the movements of foreign
diplomats and correspondents are narrowly circumscribed
and guarded.

The degree of recognizable Russian control varies in
different parts of the Soviet sphere of influence. It is smaller
in Czechoslovakia and Finland than it is in Rumania and
Bulgaria. But everywhere Moscow's power is waxing in
consequence of growing economic dependence on Russia,
growing Communist assertiveness, and attacks on the opposition by the usual dictatorial means.

The gigantic new Soviet empire in Europe and Asia was
once under Nazi, Italian, or Japanese occupation. The
Slavs, the Jews who suffered so grievously at the hands of
Hitler, the Communists, and perhaps others prefer Stalin
to Hitler. But most of them would probably be happier
without Stalin too. They cannot relish Red dictatorship in
place of brown and black. They want their personal liberties. In all the countries of the Soviet sphere, a Communist, usually Moscow trained, is minister of Interior in

charge of the secret police. All classes have fewer civil liberties now than under their prewar reactionary governments; they would certainly prefer national liberty to Moscow imperialism and the necessity of voting automatically with Russia at international assemblies. But if a democrat, Socialist, or plain person who believes in the independence of his country speaks up or acts up he may find himself in prison or in Siberia or forced to flee. Many Hungarian, Yugoslav, and Bulgarian opposition leaders had to escape to Paris and London. A few are living in Washington, D.C.

Some hardy and brave souls continue to defy the Russians and Communists in the Soviet sphere of influence. Numerous democratic "foxholes" exist in the Soviet empire, especially in Czechoslovakia, Finland, Poland, Hungary, eastern Austria, and eastern Germany. But at the moment they are without political power. The Russians and the Communists hold the empire tightly by force, repression, and economic supremacy.

It is difficult to assess the popular support that the Communists have won in the Russian orbit. In free elections, the Hungarian Communists received only 17 per cent of all votes polled. The three western zones of Germany and Berlin, voted anti-Communist overwhelmingly. So did Austria. Eastern and Central Europe have seen the Russians. They have seen the looting and raping, the transfer of machinery to Russia, the living of the Russians off the land, the confiscation of property, and the discriminatory trade treaties.

They have also seen a strange phenomenon: the moment

the war was ended, every American GI, British Tommy, French soldier, and German prisoner of war burned with eagerness to get home. Russians were the only exception to this rule of normal human behavior. Many thousands of Soviet citizens, men and women who had left their country during the war on duty or had been dragged out of it by the Nazis, have deserted and want to stay abroad. Scores of thousands of these Soviet deserters wander the face of Europe in groups or as individuals eluding the Soviet secret police or have taken refuge in American, British, and French displaced-persons camps. They have been registered and counted.

It is about these people, as well as about large numbers of Balts and Poles who do not want to go home to live under Communist rule, that Mrs. Roosevelt and Soviet Deputy Foreign Minister Vishinsky have argued at United Nations sessions in London and New York. Vishinsky demanded that they be returned to Russia against their will. Mrs. Roosevelt, as a delegate for the United States, contended that they are political exiles entitled to asylum.

"Now why," ask Europeans who know these facts, "why do these Soviet citizens prefer today's ruined, rubbled, ragged, hungry, cold Europe to their own country?"

The only possible answer is that the deserters are tired of dictatorship and hardship in Russia. Anyone who has talked to them knows that this is the answer.

That tells eastern and Central Europeans more about Russia than whole libraries of controversial books. But those inside the Soviet world cannot free themselves, and those outside frequently do not have access to the facts or are too immersed in their own troubles.

It is quite possible that the people of the Soviet world—approximately one hundred and eighty million Soviet citizens plus approximately one hundred and fifty million in the Soviet sphere of influence—three hundred and thirty million in all—yearn as much for change and relief from dictatorship as the people of the non-Soviet world desire better living conditions and truer democracy. In most countries of the Soviet world they can do little about it. In most countries of the non-Soviet world they could do a great deal.

The key to Soviet expansion is a single word: Vacuum. In Europe and Asia, Stalin has stepped in to take advantage of the power vacuum created by the defeat of Germany, Italy, and Japan, and by the postwar weakness of England and France. Equally, Russia and the Communists have stepped in everywhere throughout the world to fill the political and psychological vacuum created by a diminished faith in democracy.

The key to peace and democracy is to block further Soviet expansion by filling in the vacuums. Russia will not expand territorially if she is confronted with power instead of a power vacuum. Russia will not expand politically and ideologically if democracy is dynamic, progressive, and real.

When the people feel a spiritual emptiness, when they see no hope and are confused they will lend their ears to charlatans and their hearts to dictators. Vacuums are the playgrounds of irresponsible critics, cranks, and bullies.

The Russian problem is reminiscent of the German

problem because it stems from the same source: the failure of modern civilization to make life satisfying and ennobling. It is commonplace nowadays to say that Communism feeds on poverty. It feeds on the paucity of bread, coal, and clothes, but also on the paucity of spirit.

CHAPTER TWELVE

THE WAR OF IDEAS WITH RUSSIA

ONE World is a highly laudable ideal, and Wendell Willkie, whose early death was an American national tragedy, has a permanent niche in the hall of democratic fame for popularizing the slogan. But the world, unfortunately, is not one. It is cleft in two, and a great deal is lost by not facing this fact. Some day it will probably be one, and the question at issue is whether it will be one democratic world or one world of dictatorship. That is what all the shouting, the conferences, the speeches, and the quarrels are about.

It used to be said that Russia and America were so far from one another there could be no friction between them. But victory in the Second World War changed the map. Russia and America are today neighbors and competitors in Japan, Korea, China, Iran, Turkey, Greece, the Balkans, Austria, Germany, France, Italy, the Atlantic Ocean, and the Arctic Ocean. Russia and America are in political and ideological conflict all over the world.

Even in Latin America, where the United States has the advantage of proximity and indisputable predominance, the desire of some republics to find a balance against monopoly Yankee power (now that England is too self-absorbed to be

that balance) has of late given the Communists, and hence
Russia, a considerable accession of influence. When Dictator
Perón senses Washington hostility he flirts with Moscow,
and Moscow gladly reciprocates.

Stalin is fully aware of the political war and he is waging
it with every weapon in his arsenal. The words of the Soviet
press and radio and the deeds of Soviet officials reflect the
political war against the non-Soviet world. It is unfortunate
that so many people who write and talk about Soviet policy
cannot read Soviet magazines and newspapers.

The political war cannot be made to vanish by a wave of
the literary wand, by saying that the whole thing is a matter
of semantics, regrettable misinterpretation of words, sus-
picions, and temporary personal irritations. The political
war is visible and tangible. Every day's newspaper is a
battle bulletin of that war.

The Russians have a saying, "He went to the circus and
didn't see the elephant." The political war between the
Soviet and non-Soviet worlds is the biggest thing in international affairs. Only the blind or unintelligent do not see
it. There are those who do not want us to see it lest we fight
it and win it.

"Why compete with Russia?" is a frequent comment.
"We must get along with Russia. We must compromise and
meet Russia halfway."

The British and American governments compromised
with Russia on Poland, Germany, Austria, Yugoslavia,
Hungary, Rumania, and Bulgaria. Roosevelt and Churchill
gave Stalin half of Poland and the possibility of installing
a Moscow-made government to rule the other half from

Warsaw. Stalin was merely asked to promise "free and un-fettered elections" in Poland. He promised. He broke the promise. He promised free elections in Rumania and Bul-garia. He broke the promise. Free elections did take place in Hungary, and the Communists received only 17 per cent of the votes. But a few months later, thanks to Russian mili-tary power in Hungary, the Communist minority extended their control over the government of Hungary and gave Moscow everything it asked in the way of one-sided com-mercial treaties. At Potsdam in July and August 1945, Stalin personally promised that Germany would be treated as a single economic unit. Russia failed to fulfill the prom-ise. Stalin promised to evacuate Iran on a certain date. He stayed long beyond that date. This is what the Russians call give and take. They give a promise and they take it back.

The democracies compromised the principles of the At-lantic Charter in order to reach compromises with Russia. But it was a total loss. Stalin took what the democracies gave him and then tried to take more. This too is give and take; the democracies give and Russia takes.

The eastern half of Germany went to Russia either by direct annexation, or as a gift to Russia's puppet govern-ment in Poland, or as Russia's zone of occupation. Did that satisfy the Kremlin? No, it has since attempted to win all of Germany.

Trieste was an Italian city to which the Italians are sentimentally attached. At the cost of democracy in Italy, the democracies took Trieste away from Italy, and it has now become internationalized. But the Russian game for

Trieste has merely had its first inning. The Yugoslavs, with Moscow's blessing, are still endeavoring to draw Trieste into the Soviet sphere of influence.

Korea was divided between America and Russia. That was a compromise. But the conflict persists. The United States wants both occupying powers to leave so that the Koreans may be independent. Stalin fears that this would be the equivalent of a pro-American Korea.

The Western powers and Russia signed peace treaties for the former allies of Germany. The treaties for Finland, Rumania, Hungary, and Bulgaria confirm Russian domination of these four countries. The treaty for Italy was a setback for Italian democracy. Treaties and bargains at diplomatic conferences do not get under the surface of the Russian problem.

In spite of the innumerable compromises, concessions, and surrenders to Russia made by the Western powers since she started fighting Hitler in 1941, and especially since the end of the war, evidence of Russia's readiness to co-operate or compromise in the settlement of international political problems is microscopic, when it exists at all. The Soviet government, moreover, has remained aloof from most of the international bodies set up by the United Nations or other authorities to deal with concrete matters such as cultural and social relations, food, health, refugees, trade, credit, etc.

It is easy to say, "We must meet Russia halfway." We have met Russia 90 per cent of the way. But Russia does not meet us even 10 per cent of the way.

Moscow's reason is a very adequate one—for Moscow.

Moscow is fighting a political war with democracy. Moscow wants gains. Moscow does not want to give up anything. Moscow is keeping what she has and waiting for the opportunity—perhaps when the economic depression arrives in America—to move forward again.

The entire problem of the relations between Russia and America, or between dictatorships and the democracies, has gone beyond the field of diplomacy. The question is no longer whether Moscow and Washington can negotiate and agree. When they fall out it is seldom, if ever, about the direct, national interests of Russia or America; it is about China, Germany, Greece, Turkey, Japan, etc. Neither wants the other to conquer these countries politically. This is the political war and it cannot stop until Russia or democracy wins.

International politics has been transformed. International politics used to be the relations between governments. What persons and parties participated in the governments mattered a great deal, but was not the business of outsiders. Today, that is still true of a number of countries. But to an increasing extent, the big powers, notably Russia and America, are attempting to shape political conditions in foreign nations. For if France went Communist, she would, in effect, become a part of the Soviet sphere of influence. So Russia wants France to go Communist, and America does not want France to go Communist. Therefore, the Kremlin and the White House are equally concerned with the strength of the French Communist party, with the power which the Communists have in the French trade-union movement, and whether that movement is linked to Moscow. The same is true of Italy, of Germany, of Japan, and of many other lands. This is the new ideological imperialism which the Soviet and American governments are pursuing with vigor. (How the countries regard America's ideological or political imperialism will depend on the domestic politics of the United States.)

Tell Stalin to call off the Communist parties outside Russia? You might as well urge the United States not to sympathize with non-Communists or not to give loans and credits to governments threatened by Communists.

There are people who do actually want America to stop fighting the political war, to wash its hands of the rest of the world and live happily ever after in isolation. That would only intensify the Kremlin's expansionist drive. Russia would move into the political vacuum just as she moved into the territorial vacuum left by the collapse of Germany.

The new fact in international politics is that the Soviet world, as well as the democratic world, is engaged in ideological expansion. Ideological expansion is the equivalent of political expansion. A Communist Italy would be an asset to Russia and a setback for America and England. A democratic Japan will be anti-Communist. A Communist Germany, inevitable if America and England withdrew, would put the Russians on the Rhine looking into France. Then France would go Communist. Then the third world war would be around the corner. Or, if the remaining democracies by that time were too few and weak, it would be the end of democracy.

This was the expensive lesson of Fascist aggression and

of Pearl Harbor. Most of the old isolationists in the United States and most of the appeasers in Europe have probably learned that lesson. But now a new crop of isolationists is coming out. They are the Communists and their collaborators who cry, "Hands Off Greece," "Hands Off Turkey," "Hands Off China," "Hands Off Germany," "No Aid to Britain," etc., etc. Hands off so that Russia can put her hands on.

Since all imperialism and all expansion are bad why am I not as vehemently opposed to American expansion as I am to Soviet expansion? There is a difference: under American expansion, countries would still have the possibility of fighting for what they want, but where Russian dictatorship has spread, all opposition is ruthlessly suppressed. I am nevertheless apprehensive about American imperialism.

There are Americans who advocate the exact opposite of isolationism. They suggest an American empire and overwhelming American power throughout the world. Combat Soviet imperialism with American imperialism, they insist. I am fully convinced that this course would inevitably lead to economic disaster, revolt, and war.

Some Americans assume that Great Britain, the British Dominions, Latin America, France, Italy, Germany, Greece, Turkey, Scandinavia, the Near East, India, Indonesia, Malaya, Indo-China, China, and Japan will just jump at the idea of dependence on America for economic assistance and military protection against Russia. Why not? they say. America will save everybody from the big black wolf, or the big red bear. This is naive. They will not welcome it. They will resist it to the last. In many of those countries, to be sure, the United States could find or foster a pro-American political party. But that party would encounter much opposition.

Suspicion of America and ill will toward America already exist abroad not only among Communists and pro-Communists but among democrats who fear that the United States is the twentieth-century colossus whose enormous economic and military power will dominate lesser countries. They are worried lest conservative, capitalistic America administer aid on condition that the recipients conform to American economic and social ideas.

United States annexation of the former Japanese islands in the Pacific—officially it is not termed annexation—already troubles people in Asia and some people in America who are conscious of the importance of winning Asia's friendship. I would much rather have the friendship of a hundred million Asiatics than all the tiny coral isles of the Pacific; islands and territories will be no defense in an air-atomic war.

America's role in Europe, and in China and Japan is also being scrutinized. But propaganda distorts the picture. The fact is that the capitalist American government offered no objection to the free election of Socialists and Communists in its German zone, whereas the Soviet government did not permit the Social Democrats to operate in its zone.

The fact is that the American government favored nationalization of industries in Austria but the Soviet government obstructed it.

The fact is that General George C. Marshall did not impose a pro-American government on China as Vishinsky imposed a pro-Russian government on Rumania, as Stalin selected a pro-Russian regime for Poland. On the contrary, Marshall tried hard to introduce the anti-American, pro-Russian Communists into the Chinese government. And when his mission to end the civil war failed, he blamed not only the doctrinaire elements among the Chinese Communists, he blamed the rightist reactionaries and militarists in the Kuomintang as well. He urged China to organize a coalition government of middle-of-the-road moderates. But he did not have the power to force such a government on China.

The fact is that General MacArthur has allowed Japanese Communists, Socialists, and trade unionists practically unlimited liberty. Elections in Japan have been free. Elected governments in provinces and in Tokyo have not been dismissed by the American military occupation. Pro-Fascists, militarists, and big industrialists have been purged by MacArthur.

Yet that record, significantly, is distorted by the propagandists, and their distortions are accepted by many intelligent people. They say: "Why does America side with reaction in China? And in Greece?" "Why does America pour hundreds of millions into feudal Arab oil kingdoms?" "Is that the way to spread democracy?" American policy may look innocent to its makers in Washington, D.C., but it looks different to those who see it from the other end.

In 1946, numerous responsible Englishmen of all political parties opposed the American loan to Britain and voted in Parliament against its acceptance even though their country was desperately in need of financial assistance. The fact that

catastrophe or threatened collapse compels a foreign government to plead for and take American loans is no guarantee at all that they will be thankful or friendly.

Would an India which has gotten rid of British rule
reward America with anything but intense hostility for even
intimating that it wanted to influence India's actions at
home or abroad? Would Indonesia? Or Burma? Or Indo-
China? There are hundreds of millions of people bent on
asserting themselves, on being free.

Countries with any choice do not wish to be left alone
with a major power which may limit their national freedom.
If they suspect that the United States is launching on a new
career of imperialism, they will unite among themselves in
order to strengthen their resistance, and, in general, create
difficulties. In the end, America might have to do what
Stalin is doing: act the dictator in its sphere of influence,
set up puppet governments by force, suppress oppositions,
and banish anti-Americans to an American Siberia just as
Russia has done with the opposition leaders in Hungary,
Poland, Bulgaria, Rumania, and Yugoslavia.

Fight Stalin with Stalinism and you become stalinist.

Democratic governments and democratic organizations
should not try to beat the Communists at their own game.
They must use democratic methods and operate on democratic principles.

The powerful French Communist party, which could not
be suppressed without civil strife, influences French foreign
policy and prevents France from adopting a purely pro-
democratic, pro-Western, or pro-American foreign policy.
Arms cannot cope with that situation unless the United

States wants to police every French village and town. Getting rid of Communism in China by force alone means waging a major war in the remote Soviet Chinese areas inhabited by about one hundred and fifty million people. Can America do that? Is it ready to do it? I think the answer is No.

The "realism" which says you must stop Soviet imperialism with a bigger and better American imperialism is not realism at all; it is foolish and self-defeating.

Democracy is under attack. Now is the time, therefore, to be more democratic, more moral, more Christian, more gandhian. This is the only hope of victory over dictatorship. A democracy that is untrue to itself—especially in crisis—will wreck itself.

Neither American isolationism nor British isolationism is the answer to Russian expansion. Some innocent Englishmen imagine there will be neutrals in the first atomic war; they imagine they can remain democratic while Russia expands or while Russia and America are fighting it out for supremacy. But England has the key position in the war for democracy. Without England, democracy may be destroyed. Nor will England's world position improve if her statesmen deliberately spoil their relations with the United States. That will merely put Britain at the mercy of a Russia which will be encouraged to expand by England's coldness toward America. Isolation is as obsolete for England as it is for the United States.

Nor is American imperialism the answer to Russian imperialism. That means struggle, clash, trouble.

Nor is the atomic bomb. Certain vocal Americans would drop atomic bombs on Moscow tomorrow afternoon. Friends of democracy? No. They are enemies of democracy. They have no faith in democracy. They do not believe that democracy could win in peaceful competition with Soviet dictatorship.

I do.

So let the democracies and Russia compete. If Russia wins, there will be no democracies. If the democracies win the political war with Russia, there will be no shooting war.

The entire non-Soviet world, not merely the United States, must fight the political war against Soviet Russia. I think the democracies could win if they pursued the correct strategy of victory. What is that strategy?

CHAPTER THIRTEEN

A PLAN FOR PREVENTING WAR
WITH RUSSIA

THE world is in a sad mess. Economic misery may engulf the globe. There could be a third world war with millions of casualties. Democracy itself may die. This is not pessimism. It is merely the truth. The pessimist says nothing can be done about it. The pessimist laughs it off, is full of false gaiety, reads murder stories, and gets drunk. The optimist is solemn. The optimist is a Jeremiah. He thinks something *can* be done.

The third world war can be prevented. There is no such thing as an inevitable war. Wars don't happen; they are made. The making of the Second World War is recorded in print for all to read. Wars are made by a million stupidities. They can be prevented by wisdom, vision, and timely action.

The democracies are always ready to fight wars "to make the world safe for democracy." They fought the First World War and the Second World War "to make the world safe for democracy." But then they do nothing between the wars "to make the world safe for democracy," and so they have to fight another war "to make the world safe for democracy."

We may be fighting a war with Russia in ten or fifteen years to save the world from dictatorship unless we start right now saving the world from dictatorship by peaceful means.

You either fight for democracy during the peace or you fight for democracy in a war.

How do you fight for democracy in peacetime?

By being democratic.

The democracies have a number of years—perhaps ten—in which to stop the descent into the first atomic war. If at the end of that time Russian-American relations are as tense and unsatisfactory as they are now a war would be very likely, for America's present postwar antiwar mood would have evaporated and Russia's present inability to fight might be ended. (Stalin has estimated fifteen years as the period necessary to restore Soviet economy from the ravages of the Second World War.)

In the next decade, the democracies must extend and enrich democracy everywhere. This is the only way of avoiding a war with the Soviet empire.

The democracies must have the will to improve democracy, and they must have a concrete plan.

The plan for saving democracy by enriching it should not be drawn up exclusively by American statesmen or carried out by Americans alone. Americans live too well, are too far away, and have too much faith in capitalist enterprise to grasp the depth of the difficulty which confronts the world. "Free enterprise and freedom are wonderful, are they not? Why change? Everything would be fine if it were not for Russia." So all they can propose is "Be tough with Russia" and "Prohibit the Communist party." It is that attitude which handicaps conservatives and reactionaries in dealing adequately with the world's biggest problems. They do not know how bad the trouble is.

The situation is so serious that it needs an epic solution. But many of the statesmen seem to have reached a dead end and so have most men who are caught in the web of national power. It is pitiful to watch high officials discussing whether a frontier should be ten miles to the east or eight miles to the west; they should be discussing the abolition of national frontiers. It is even more distressing to find governments debating how much industrial production should be permitted in Germany. When millions throughout the earth are starved, sick, weak, and dying because goods are scarce, the stoppage of production for any reason is a crime. Yet apparently sane persons have contemplated such a policy for Germany. They are afraid Germany may make another war. This is a confession of man's incapacity to control the power which his ingenuity has conjured up out of the earth, the air, the water, and himself.

These statesmen have brains. But they are in the grip of outmoded notions. They are trying to pour the second half of the twentieth century into nineteenth century molds; it doesn't work. They are squeezing the world of jet aviation and atomics into the old corset of nationalism; hence the shrieks of pain.

Democracy can only be saved by internationalism.

Take the Ruhr as an illustration. The Ruhr is the richest and most important industrial region in Europe. It is the industrial heart of Europe. But in the past it beat only for

Germany, and since it was too big for her, Germany went in search of the entire body and twice attempted to conquer Europe.

What to do now? Cut out half the heart and throw it away, thus wasting precious production and killing many human beings? That was suggested by some governments. Give the Ruhr to France? The heart would be too big for France, and Germany would be left without even a pulse. France nevertheless demanded just this. Or unite the heart with the entire body, with Europe, so that the Ruhr will pump blood for Germany, and for France, and for all Europe? This would be economic internationalism. Good business, good management, good markets, and plain humanity, as well as peace, require economic internationalism in many places on the earth's surface. Nationalism is simply inefficient and out of date.

Nation-by-nation patchwork, whether economic or political, is no good. The United States hurriedly gave a loan to France when Léon Blum, the French Socialist leader, visited Washington in 1946 on the eve of the French elections. America did not want the Communists to sweep the polls. The loan was probably necessary. But that is no way of contending with a world-wide difficulty or even with French difficulties. For the loan was granted and still the difficulties persist.

The social, political, and economic fabric tears in Greece. So Greece gets a loan. The fabric seems to be getting thin in Turkey. Turkey gets a loan. But the fabric may tear anywhere, for it is the same threadbare fabric that has been worn and patched too much.

India needs steel. If India could buy steel mills from America, Indians would earn more money and might buy more French goods. If the French consequently bought more Greek tobacco, if the Ruhr produced without hindrance and bought more Greek tobacco, if Greek ships carried bigger cargoes, and if Greece's northern Slav neighbors stopped interfering in Greek affairs, then maybe Greece could get a middle-of-the-road government and settle down. Perhaps the Greek problem must first be dealt with outside of Greece.

Often national problems depend on international treatment. Often economic problems are basic and yet cannot be tackled until the political hurdles are removed.

The point is a very simple one: The job cannot be done piecemeal. It cannot be done by a bank. It cannot be done by one government. To improve democracy and thereby prevent war, an international organization is required with political plus economic powers. This is the heart of the strategy of democratic victory. An international organization with political and economic powers is an international government.

It sounds drastic and revolutionary. It is. But the world will continue to flounder without it. We will potter and patch and lose time, but get it in the end anyway. We have already commenced to move in the direction of international government.

A number of objections are heard against international government:

Objection number one: "People are not ready for internationalism; the world is more nationalistic than ever."

This seems logical but isn't. The growing nationalism of today comes from fear and insecurity. It in turn causes fear and insecurity, thus feeding on itself and getting bigger and worse all the time. To arrive at internationalism you cannot wait till nationalism tapers off. Of itself it will never taper off. It will only taper off when there is internationalism. Internationalism helps bring security, and security eliminates fear. No fear, no nationalism. The international government will reduce nationalism and thereby reduce the danger of war.

Objection number two: "How can anyone who wants democracy and is afraid of power monopolies favor a super-government which, by its very scope and duties, would have to exercise tremendous power?"

The world is witnessing the extension of American and Russian power and the contraction of the independence of many weaker countries. This will continue, and all lesser nations may become battlefields on which the two major powers contend for supremacy, unless an international authority is established to safeguard the weak against the mighty. In the absence of international government, one nation—it could only be America or Russia—will command the earth and subordinate all other nations to it. That indeed would be a super supergovernment with unlimited power. Before this tragedy occurs, and while they still have freedom of action, the democracies, big and small, should unite in an international union. The union government would enjoy certain rights, but so would the governments of the members of the union, the present nations. Checks and balances would restrain the strong; regional confederation in Europe, Asia, Latin America, and Africa could question any excessive arrogation of power by the international administration which, in any case, would not deal with all phases of human affairs. This is the best chance of survival the nonmajor powers have, and since international government is the only chance of preserving democracy and peace it should also appeal to the United States.

Objection number three: "Why is Russia deliberately excluded from the proposed government?"

Russia is excluded because she will not help reinforce capitalist democracy, mixed economy, or Social Democracy. Bolshevism is opposed, in theory and in practice, to capitalist democracy, mixed economy and Social Democracy. Its spokesmen and friends detest and attack these forms. Then how can Russia be expected to reinforce them?

The democratic world must, to avoid war and to perpetuate itself, solve the problems of democracy. The Soviet dictatorship, naturally, has no desire to participate in the solution of these problems. It has, on the contrary, aggravated them in Germany, China, Greece, almost everywhere.

The democratic world is in its present confused and depressed state because it has delayed necessary changes and improvements. The delay has given Communism a golden opportunity to expand. Now the democracies must change and improve, and thereby check Communism. But Russia is not in the business of checking Communism.

The diplomats exhaust themselves talking with Russia about establishing the kind of world and the kind of institutions in which, they hope, democracy would thrive and Communism would shrivel. Do they really suppose Moscow will co-operate in that task? Do they really believe their conferences and bargains alter the fundamental desire of Russia to spread Communism or their own desire, as democrats, to stem Communism?

Russia and the democracies want opposite things. How can they walk together? For peace? Peace is not a condition of frozen attitudes. Nations struggle with one another in peacetime. They always have. They are doing so now. Today, the struggle is very intense. The fact that in any given moment the world is at peace does not mean that the peace is not being undermined. Peace might mean, often has meant, that the world was moving toward war. The world —with the exception of Spain and China—was at peace in 1937 and 1938. But it was not peace; and if the democracies had known it was not peace, they might have done something to prevent the Second World War.

So it is not enough to say, "I want peace." You must want the kind of peace which is not the prelude to war, nor the preparation for war. We are going to have peace for a number of years in any case: a peace of physical and spiritual exhaustion. What will be happening during this interval? If it is to be filled with a war of political ideas then it is not peace and we might as well recognize it.

The man who cries, "Peace. Peace," must declare himself on the vital question of political war. Does he suggest that the democracies strengthen democracy throughout the world? If his answer is No, then he favors the spread of Communism, and that must end in war or in the end of democracy. If his answer is Yes, if he wants to fight the political war for democracy against Communism then he cannot fight that war together with Communist Russia or Communist Yugoslavia or the Russian colonies.

The Soviet government has given few, if any, concrete indications of its readiness to co-operate in the solution of the world's peacetime political, military, economic, social, or cultural problems. When we stop talking generalities and get down to actual cases of co-operation, they are difficult, indeed practically impossible to find. The fiction that the world is one should therefore not be allowed to postpone the unification and improvement of world democracy.

Two families occupying the same house might live on excellent terms. But if they began quarreling about whose turn it was to sweep up or who was using too much gas it might be better for their friendship if one moved to another house.

Shoemakers are not eligible to membership in a society of atomic scientists. Fascists are not accepted in a liberal association. Liberals are not accepted in a Communist party. Exclusion based on prejudice or sordid self-interest is indecent. But exclusion based on divergence of ideas or of functions is an everyday, inescapable fact.

The exclusion of the Soviet Union from the international government does not grow out of hostility to the Soviet peoples. It is simply a recognition of different interests and functions which, on the record, have militated against Russia's collaboration with the non-Soviet world.

The creation of an international government of the democratic world without Russia will prove of great advantage to the inhabitants of the Soviet Union. For if the democracies begin to understand that peace requires a democratic solution of their own difficulties and if, instead of engaging in irritating, futile negotiations with Moscow, they formed a union for resolving those difficulties they would give up any false notion that their future safety and happiness dictate a war with Russia. The international government, moreover, would prevent Russia from capturing weak countries. The international government would be stronger than Russia. By thus thwarting Russian expansion, the third world war would be prevented. A prolonged period of peace would bring democracy into Russia.

Today, the tensions and irritations between the democratic world and Russia are great, and growing. They are dangerous. All this is due to the fact that the two worlds live in one house and are trying to solve the insoluble problems created by that common life. Let them separate, and trade relations and diplomatic relations with Russia will improve.

Fear of Russia, hostility toward Russia, and consideration of war with Russia would cease if the democracies had an instrument to deal with their own shortcomings. They would concentrate on this task. Success would mean peace.

Peace depends not on armaments and not on diplomacy. It depends on economic, political, and moral self-improvement, and on internationalism.

Objection number four: "What about the United Nations? Will not an international government take the place of and therefore destroy the UN?"

The United States government, fearing that the American public might oppose membership in the UN and thereby handicap it as similar abstention handicapped the League of Nations, immoderately oversold it in its propaganda during 1944 and 1945. Exaggerated hopes have therefore been invested in the UN. The organization has valuable uses, but it is not equipped to handle major political or economic questions. Already, so early in its life, statesmen are treating it as governments did the League of Nations, and for the same reason. They ignore it. It was the big powers that sabotaged the oil and other League sanctions against Fascist Italy. After that failure, the Spanish issue was placed in the lap of the London Non-Intervention Committee which vulgarly perverted its purpose and helped Franco to victory. Though the League of Nations was in session during the height of the Czechoslovak crisis in September 1938, the issue was reserved for the untender mercies of Neville Chamberlain and Edouard Daladier who rushed to the altar at Munich and slaughtered the lamb.

Today, in the same way, really crucial issues are handled outside the UN because the UN has no money, no police force, no sovereignty, no power.

Its biggest drawback is the veto. According to the text of the San Francisco Charter, which was lauded as the tollgate to heaven, only the Security Council of the UN can prevent war by taking action against the aggressor. The Security Council consists of eleven members: the Big Five (the United States, the Soviet Union, Great Britain, France, and China), who are permanent members, and six small or medium nations elected for short terms. Each of the permanent powers has the right of veto. Suppose one of the Big Five committed an act of aggression. The other ten members of the jury might vote Guilty, but the eleventh, the criminal aggressor himself, votes No, and so the UN, as the UN, could do nothing. Its members would have to act outside, thus breaking up the UN, in order to act for peace. The veto is, obviously, an evil manifestation of national sovereignty. A nation with power is above the law. It is sovereign.

It is supremely significant that the veto was inserted in the San Francisco Charter on the insistence of the United States, the most powerful nation, and Russia, the nation most addicted to power. It is the Soviet government, however, that has used the veto in the UN on numerous occasions, not the United States.

Power can be curbed by law backed by organized force. The strong nation has least need of law enforcement for its own protection and least desire to have the law protect its possible victim.

The United States has displayed a readiness to give up some of its veto power. The governments of many countries —China, Australia, Holland, New Zealand, Great Britain, etc.—and many large organizations and prominent individuals have publicly attacked the veto as detrimental to peace. But the Soviet government has fought fiercely against any limitation on the veto and has excoriated anyone who criticized its use. Spokesmen of the Soviet government have vigorously defended the concept of national sovereignty. That is natural in view of Russia's new nationalism at home. When the Soviets were less nationalistic at home they did not defend national sovereignty so strongly.

The veto should be abolished. That would be a long step toward making the UN a truly effective international government.

Some contend that without the veto the Soviet Union would always find itself outvoted by a combination of capitalist nations. With the veto, Russia can block all the other powers. In other words, according to this strange doctrine, it is wrong for a majority to outvote Russia, but it is fine for Russia alone to outvote the majority. This is the arithmetic, and logic, of dictatorship. It is nationalism gone berserk and Bolshevik. If Russia feels the unalterable hostility of the non-Soviet powers how is the UN ever going to function?

The veto must be abandoned. Should Russia rebel, she is free to withdraw from the United Nations. She would always be welcomed back when she was prepared to accept the only basis on which an international organization can work: internationalism.

Russia's Foreign Commissar Maxim Litvinov was the foremost champion and symbol of collective security until Stalin dismissed him in 1939 just at the moment when Moscow began its present career of expansion. As chief Soviet delegate to the League of Nations in Geneva, Litvinov regularly attacked the idea of "universality." He did not believe in universality or unanimity because it enabled Germany, Italy, or Japan to paralyze the League. Litvinov, for instance, consciously maneuvered Italy out of the Nyon conference, September 1937, which was convened to discuss the predatory act of Mussolini's "unknown" submarines against ships carrying supplies to Loyalist Spain. Litvinov knew that Italy's presence would naturally disrupt the meeting. Italy was not present, the remaining participants consequently agreed, and for a while an Anglo-French naval patrol succeeded in stopping Fascist piracy in the Mediterranean.

The veto implies universality, unanimity, and a whip in the hand of the aggressive, lawless nation. It is the dictatorship of one nation ruled by one man. That kind of UN cannot save democracy. Stalin is not yearning to save democracy.

The lesser commissions and persons in the UN valiantly try to employ it for good purposes. The League had such commissions and persons. But the top-rank statesmen have generally used the UN to embarrass each other.

What is the sense of a UN that can do nothing to cure the major ills on earth? Better a UN with Russia, if Russia proves she loves peace and freedom. But better a UN without Russia, if Russia obstructs, as she has been obstructing in and outside of the UN, the measures our world earnestly needs in order to escape death.

Unless the UN is converted into an instrument to improve democracy, Russia will employ it as a weapon to divide and ultimately crush the democracies.

Without delay, the UN's charter has to be amended and the UN thereby transformed into an effective international government to advance prosperity, personal freedom, and peace.

The UN is not an international government. It must be remade to become one. It is very likely that the moment the nations begin reshaping the UN they will be on the way to an international government without Russia. This is regrettable. But what is the alternative? Refrain from establishing an international government and thereby deprive ourselves of a desperately needed means of saving peace and democracy? That is too high a price to pay for Russia's formal, obstructionist membership in the UN.

Without an international government, humanity will drift, as it is drifting today, toward chaos. Such a state of affairs would foster American imperialism and Russian imperialism, and, ultimately, a war between them. That is a very excessive price to pay for Russian unco-operation in the UN.

Giving birth to an international government would be easier than it seems. A large number of UN agencies that cope with concrete tasks are already at work, and Russia is not in them. Other international agencies are needed. The United States government's official Baruch Plan for the control of atomic energy envisaged the formation of an Atomic Development Authority (ADA) to manage all deposits of uranium and other fissionable materials throughout the world, to be the sole manufacturer of atomic bombs, and the sole user of atomic bombs in case of need. The Russians passionately rejected it. Ambassador Gromyko, speaking for Stalin, declared the ADA was superfluous; just let America scrap all its atomic bombs and stop making more. And how would anybody know whether Russia, or Argentina, or Spain, or Turkey was not making bombs secretly? Would Russia permit unhindered inspection inside her territories? The Kremlin several times gave the vague impression that it might admit limited inspection. But limited inspection is not inspection, and Russia's answer, therefore, was No. A dictatorship cannot allow outsiders, or even its own citizens, to move freely and look around.

In an address delivered in New York on May 19, 1947, Andrei A. Gromyko, Soviet Deputy Foreign Minister, objected to unlimited inspection because "it cannot be reconciled with the sovereignty and independence of states." He added, "The United Nations is an organization of sovereign states. The undermining of the sovereignty and independence of its members is the destruction of the basis of its existence." But sovereignty is also the basis of the impotence of the United Nations in dealing with threats of war.

Russia's rejection of the Baruch Plan for the control of atomic bombs caused a turning point in American foreign policy. It led to Truman's declaration regarding the need of saving Greece and Turkey from Communist expansion. If Russia fears America's possession of the atomic bomb she should have accepted the Baruch scheme under which the United States, as well as all countries, could neither have nor make atomic bombs.

But the Baruch Plan would have made it forever impossible for Russia to manufacture atomic bombs. That did not suit Moscow.

The Soviet government wants to have the atomic bomb. Rather than surrender the right to possess it the Kremlin resigns itself to American possession of the bomb. Why? There are several possible reasons: Stalin knows that a democracy, especially America, whose people have a guilty conscience about the use of the bomb against Hiroshima and Nagasaki, would be unlikely to drop atomic missiles on peaceful countries. Stalin is not afraid of America's atomic bombs. But he probably thinks that the bomb in Russia's hands would give Russia an advantage over the United States, whose greater density of population, big cities, and concentrated industrial centers make it more vulnerable to attack. Finally, Stalin has shown no faith in international control of anything. He believes in national power rather than in international organization.

Russia's refusal to outlaw the atomic bomb through internationalism was a serious setback to the One World idea and, together with the other numerous signs of Soviet unco-operativeness, make it desperately urgent to prevent an atomic war by fighting the political war.

The first step toward victory in this political war is the establishment of an international government.

The international government would administer the Atomic Development Authority; under it all nations, including backward nations very much in need of new sources of industrial energy, would soon have access to atomic power as well as the protection of an agency with a store of atomic bombs.

The international government would have a police force. It would run the international bank that is already set up. It would administer the Ruhr. It would build TVA's on the Yangtze, the Rhine, and other rivers. It would regulate international trade without tariffs. It would foster the exchange of cultural values. (The UN has the UNESCO for this purpose but Russia has not joined it.) It would, one hopes, defend human rights. It would supervise international waterways (Dardanelles, Suez, Gibraltar, Panama, the Rhine, etc.), thus eliminating jealousies and quarrels.

It would exercise the important functions which no national government can perform.

The international government would be a factor in diminishing the power of national governments. It would thus decrease the likelihood of national dictatorships. Moreover, it would, in the Ruhr for instance, own the major industrial installations. Most Europeans would certainly prefer that to ownership by an international cartel or by American capital.

From its economic activities, the international government would get enough revenue to pay its running expenses.

In this first stage, the international government would be a pool of the sovereignty assigned to it by separate nations. It would consist of the UN agencies and the various international authorities, linked together.

But a government is really not a government unless it is elected by people and unless it then makes laws binding on those people. That is the logic of the proposal made in the House of Commons on November 23, 1945, by British Foreign Secretary Ernest Bevin. It was an historic proposal. He said, "We need a new study for the purpose of creating a world assembly elected directly by the people of the world, as a whole, to whom the governments who form the United Nations are responsible and who, in fact, make the world law which they, the people, will then accept and be morally bound and willing to carry out. For it will be from their votes that the power will have been derived, and it will be for their direct representatives to carry it out."

That is internationalism and it is also saturated with democracy. Moscow therefore bitterly opposes such ideas.

A few weeks after Bevin spoke, former Foreign Secretary Anthony Eden made a similar suggestion, and thereupon the Moscow radio denounced Bevin and Eden and scoffed at their "world parliament" as "merely utopian" and "harmful and reactionary" to boot.

The Soviet government is quite consistent in all this. How could a dictatorship allow its people to vote freely for a world parliament—presumably with rival parties and rival candidates—when they cannot vote freely for their national parliament?

These are the reasons why only democracies can start moving toward international government. If they wait for Russia they will never start and Russia could then keep the democratic world permanently divided—which is just what she wants. Democratic division helps Moscow undermine democracy.

With Russia, international government is practically impossible. Without Russia it becomes practically possible.

The international government would offer such obvious and overwhelming material and defense advantages that most countries not under Moscow's thumb would voluntarily join. But they could also go their own way until the international government's advantages convinced them of the wisdom of membership. Any satellite of Russia could likewise adhere and thereby acquire protection against Moscow's vengeance. Some day, a democratic Russia could adhere.

The launching of the international government would instantly alter the whole atmosphere and temper of the democratic world. It would be a tonic to individuals and nations. Today's perpetual fear of the next war is going to make men and women and countries sick unless they soon see a working arrangement that promises to prevent war and remove its causes. Only an international government can do that.

An international government would reduce the strength of Communism in the democratic world. Everywhere, Communists are nationalists. They pose as defenders of their countries against foreign dangers. It brings them adherents. In France, for instance, the Communists claim that they stand guard against Germany and that a Communist France, linked with Communist Russia, would end the German menace. It would also end democracy in France. But an international government would guarantee French security against Germany; it would foster German-French economic co-operation and thus destroy the heritage of hate between the two countries; it would guarantee French prosperity. The relaxation would weaken the Communists.

Nationalism, separatism, fear of war, and preparations for war help Communism. Communists preach violence as a doctrine; they use violence. They are adept in its use. They were the leaders in the anti-Fascist resistance movements in Europe. They do not shrink from violence in strikes. They encourage and take advantage of interreligious violence in India. They are the children of force and flourish in an atmosphere of conflict.

We live in a violent era and it confers benefits on Communists and Fascists who believe in violence as a legitimate means. Let democracy, by peaceful methods, settle the problems between countries and within countries, and Communism will wither away.

International government would have the same effect on order, security, and morality as the advent of a government with adequate police power in a wild-west frontier town which had been at the mercy of a gang of two-gun desperadoes. Business and personal life would become normal; individual and public decency would rise. Tensions would disappear. The non-Soviet world and, I am convinced, the people of Russia would sigh with relief.

Sabers and shotguns did not win the Second World War. Neither can obsolete ideas win the political war for democracy. In the age of atomics, electronics, and jet propulsion, internationalism is inescapable. Politics must keep step with science.

It was quite fitting for Russia, the Communist parties, and Fascism to adopt nationalism. Nationalism promotes the fears, hates, and irrational passions on which dictatorships feed.

Nationalism is designed to make Soviet citizens conscious of the difference between themselves and the outside world. Any idea like the brotherhood of man would kill Stalinism.

When Stalin forsook internationalism for nationalism he also restored the unenlightened Greek Orthodox Church of Russia and tried to weave a mystic halo around feudal knights and princes and czars. They all go together.

National communism is the reactionary past; it could not withstand progressive international democracy any more than rifles can stop atomic bombs.

A struggle between American nationalism and Russian

nationalism must end in the victory of one nationalism and in one country's dictatorship over the world. But a struggle between international democracy and national communism could only end in the victory of international democracy because all the forces of progress, sanity, and freedom would be united behind it.

To win, democracy must make sure that it does actually represent progress, sanity, and freedom. An international government of the democracies would stand for all three, and strength besides.

CHAPTER FOURTEEN

TURN THE SEARCHLIGHT INWARD

THE task facing the democratic world is to achieve union and to enrich the content of democracy. That will make it immune to attacks of Stalinism from within or from without. This is the peaceful way, the best way, and probably the only way of preventing the third world war. This is also the way of improving relations with Soviet Russia.

Atomic energy and aviation are cracking the old concept of nation states. Atomic energy may indeed be explosive in many senses. It may transform the economic system. The rise of the colonial peoples is likewise changing the shape of things. The democratic world is due for reform. Russia is merely hastening the process.

I do not think that Bolshevik Russia, with her imperialism, nationalism, dictatorship, and relative cultural, industrial, and scientific backwardness has much to offer to the non-Soviet world.

The typical Russian, whether czarist or soviet—a generalization but largely correct—both loves and hates Europe. He fears and respects the foreigner. He tries to copy Europe yet wants to destroy it. I would not want Russia to have power over Europe; I would not want to see Europe russianized. I would rather see Russia europeanized. Lenin started the process. The original purpose of Bolshevism was to turn Russia to Europe. Bolshevism was a revolt against the past. Then Stalin embraced that past and perverted his cause. Now Russia is poised to crush Europe by enslaving it. That would be Russia's and the world's loss.

What has Russia which Asia needs? Discipline? Russia has no discipline. Discipline is self-imposed. Russia has regimentation, which is superimposed. The Chinese or Indian has more discipline than the Soviet citizen. The Russian of today is incapable of the discipline of gandhian civil disobedience. Land reform? Asia is pining for land reform, but stalinist collectivization has become a new form of serfdom; more regimentation. Dynamism? Yes, there is movement, noise, power in Russia. To what purpose? Not the flowering of the individual.

If Stalin ruled Asia he would squeeze the spirit out of the best in Asia—Mahatma Gandhi. Those Asiatics who look to Moscow, and those who get their inspiration from totalitarian Japan, are the least gandhian, the most antigandhian. They are the callow, amateur militarists, the saluting slogan shouters. They think they are behaving like free men, or that this is the way to achieve freedom. This is the way to lose both personal and national freedom. By following stalinist methods they can only lose to Stalin who perfected them.

Communist shock-brigade, smash-through tactics often have a fatal lure for weak persons or for liberals and laborites who feel they are accomplishing too little. These people are sometimes tempted to imitate the organizational methods and "discipline" of totalitarians; the huge, loud meetings, the marching battalions, the strident, exaggerated propaganda, and the unbridled denunciations of opponents. Just so, new Asiatic governments and perhaps unstable European governments may think they will succeed if they flex their muscles, use force brutally, and prove their "dynamism" by showing how quickly and energetically they can meet situations.

Beneath all the social, economic, and political problems of the democracies is one root problem: the moral problem, the problem of decent relations between countries and between persons, and here Russia has little or nothing to contribute; Stalinism is immoral.

Democracy can learn from Mahatma Gandhi rather than from Generalissimo Stalin. In Gandhi, democracy could find the impulse to be loyal to the best in itself. To follow Stalin, democracy would have to cease being itself.

Democracy was always imperfect yet managed to do well. But now it is under severe attack and it is like a body fighting a germ: the body must be at its best, get new vitamins, open up pockets of reserve strength. The precious freedoms of a democracy—and only those who never lived in a dictatorship will scoff at these—have to be expanded and supplemented. For the Russian challenge has made men critical. It is a strange situation: the Soviet Union has neither political nor economic democracy. The Bolsheviks live in a glass house. Yet they throw stones. They can do it because their glass house is protected by an iron curtain and nobody can throw any stones which will reach the Soviet people. Communist and Soviet criticism of Western democracy, and criticism which is not inspired by either, have nevertheless impelled people to look more closely at the contents of democracy. They look more closely and demand more improvement.

Democracy might profit from Gandhi's suggestion: "Turn the searchlight inward."

The democratic world as a whole should turn the searchlight inward. It ought to ask itself some searching questions: Can democracy fight dictatorship when there are dictatorships like Franco's in its own midst? Was it democratic for the Big Three or Four to decide the fate of small countries without even consulting them? Is it democratic to give active or passive aid to a dictatorship that wants to swallow an independent nation? Is it democratic for major powers to seek their own security at the expense of the security of minor powers; don't they know there is no security in territory? Is the big-power veto in the United Nations democratic? Is it democratic to stem the surge of colonies toward freedom? Does "Might is Right" stand for democracy or the jungle? Will diplomats stop applying the term "peace-loving" loosely to all countries that went to war when they were attacked by the Axis and apply it only to nations that are concretely ready to merge part of their national sovereignty in an international government?

The democratic world cannot prosper unless the British Labor government succeeds. All the gold and goods of America will not suffice to stem Communism in the Eastern Hemisphere without the close and equal co-operation of England in Europe and of India in Asia. Communism will not be defeated in Europe and Asia unless the United States adopts a friendly, or at least a tolerant attitude toward Socialist and mixed economy regimes. Now that the threat of unemployment in England has been superseded by a long-range manpower shortage, the British trade unions must cease their opposition to immigration of foreign workers. France must awaken to the fact that an unproductive, unhappy, sick Germany will ultimately lead to a Russo-German union that will dominate Europe, France included. Germans should show by their behavior and votes that they do not want to be Russia's cat's-paws. Australia, her exemplary foreign policy notwithstanding, excludes colored immigrants. This is neither democratic nor helpful to world democracy. South Africa's discrimination against colored peoples weakens Asia's faith in democracy. Hindus and Moslems would do well to start thinking as citizens of India and of the world. The Chinese national government cannot defeat the Communists with arms alone; the Chinese Communists will win friends among the land-hungry peasants as long as the Kuomintang party and the central government are honeycombed with landlords and warlords who obstruct the land reform and encourage bribery, speculation, and bureaucratic inefficiency.

All these requirements might be met more readily if the democratic world has an international government. In such a government the best democracies would set an example for the others.

Each democratic country should turn the searchlight inward. The limitation of franchise by prejudice and fear is not democracy. Democracy is mocked where a Catholic or a Jew cannot be elected to office, where only rich men or "aristocrats" are eligible to diplomatic posts or other positions, where rich men and unscrupulous, corrupt politicians control a political party, and where persons elected to be representatives of the people listen too intently to highly paid lobbyists.

Does a government expel residents who belong to a minority race? Does it deny the right of asylum to the oppressed and imperiled? That government is infringing a democratic principle.

It is easy to give freedom to those who agree with us. The test of democracy is the freedom of those who disagree. Are individuals or groups persecuted for the ideas they hold and do they find it difficult or impossible to express them? That is Stalinism. That is what Hitler, Mussolini, and the Japanese did. Franco does it. Let Paul Robeson say or sing anything he pleases. You lessen his criticisms of democracy by giving him democratic freedoms. He could not talk or sing against Stalinism in Russia. You tell him that, and tell his friends that, and you may make converts to democracy. In any case, you cannot believe in freedom and deny freedom.

No man is completely free who is starving, or unemployed, or unable to get an education if he wants it. Slums that create bad health, crime, and immorality are not democratic. A democracy that underpays its teachers is not serving democracy. Fear of an old age without funds often produces tensions, greed, ethical corruption and speculation in middle-aged persons and thus operates against morality in democracy.

Even the freest elections and full freedom of speech and

assembly will not guarantee democracy in the presence of widespread material want and insecurity.

Nor is a man completely free when his race or religion is persecuted. In a new suburb near the Los Angeles airport I saw a large sign reading GOOD RESTRICTIONS. That means no Jews or Negroes admitted. That is Hitlerism. How can it be "good"? It is un-Christian. How can it be democratic?

Eliminate that which is totalitarian in democracy and you cut the ground from under the feet of its domestic and foreign enemies. Do nothing constructive and instead shout "Reds" at Communists or at others and you make Communists. Behave like Hitler and you make Nazis and Fascists as well as Communists.

If each democracy looked at itself critically, coldly, to discover its undemocratic flaws and then eradicated them, democracy would not be at a crisis the world over.

Each man, woman, and child in every democracy should follow Gandhi's precept and turn the searchlight inward. That can be as concrete as each individual wishes to make it.

At a dinner meeting in Long Beach, California, I talked about the political war against Stalin's Russia and recalled Gandhi's feeling that the modern world concentrates too much on "getting" and too little on "being." "Stop and be," is the Mahatma's philosophy. After the proceedings, a man came up who introduced himself as a physician.

"What can the average citizen do?" he asked, somewhat troubled.

"Well," I said, "you receive fifty-five or eighty patients a day."

"I'm going to reduce my fees," he declared.

The doctor understood the political war for democracy.

Up on Central Park West in New York, one evening, I stopped to watch two young boys shoveling heavy, freshly fallen snow from a pavement in front of a store. They worked diligently, but when one straightened his back for a moment, I asked, "Who got you to do this?" The store was closed.

He said, "Nobody, we're doing it for nothing."

I offered them some coins. "No, thanks," they said, "we're Boy Scouts."

Will they be just as ready to serve the community when they are grown up, or will "life," which means the mad rush to "get," spoil them? Aren't there more good children than good adults?

Newspaper editorials condemn school teachers for organizing trade unions and going out on strike. "A school teacher is a public servant." The newspaper, the magazine, the radio, the book publishing company has as important a social function for adults as the teacher has for children. Does the newspaper owner regard himself as a public servant? Or does he feel that his chief concern is not to inform, educate, and elevate, but to amuse and please his readers and sell papers?

Most individuals shirk social responsibility. Citizens of a democracy usually feel that their duty is done when they cast a ballot. And if they send a telegram to a congressman or keep a watchful eye on the government and protest against its blunders, they congratulate themselves on their civic virtue. But democracy is more than free elections and good government.

Mahatma Gandhi says the persons immediately concerned should deal with a situation before it becomes so grave that it demands official attention. He believes, in other words, in self-help and co-operative effort rather than in passing a law. His is the extreme view: laws sometimes help. But you cannot legislate brotherly love or truth or charity or fair play or tolerance. Because democracy is on the statute books is no sufficient reason for regarding it as a living fact. Only living beings can, by their hour-to-hour conduct, make it a living fact.

Gandhi has no hate, no envy, no venom, no resentments. For thirty years he fought British imperialism without ever uttering a bitter word against any Englishman. He remained a friend of the very viceroys who jailed him. He opposed a system, not individuals. His method made him invulnerable. It gave him tremendous impact.

"I am no lover of the landlord system," Gandhi told a prayer meeting in the province of Bihar in March 1947, "I have often spoken against it. But I confess frankly that I am not an enemy of landlords. I own no enemies. The best way to bring about reform in the economic and social systems, whose evils are admittedly many, is through the royal road of self-suffering. Any departure from it only results in merely changing the form of the evil that was sought to be liquidated violently."

During the same tour in Bihar, undertaken to castigate Hindus for maltreating Moslems, Gandhi told a prayer meeting that he had received a letter which abused him. "If a man abuses me," he declared, "it would never do for me to return the abuse. An evil returned by another evil only succeeds in multiplying it instead of leading to its reduction. It is a universal law that violence cannot be quenched by superior violence. . . ."

How often one hasty word ends in a big quarrel and estrangement because the persons involved cannot forgive, unwind, relax! How often the man with a little power, abused by somebody with more power, vents his resentments on somebody with no power! How often the persecuted try to become persecutors! How much ugliness grows out of the desire to prove one's superiority or to demonstrate one's authority! How many useful organizations are wrecked or weakened because people passionately devoted to the same cause are envious of one another's positions!

Gandhi humiliates himself whenever public service demands it. That is his strength. He is always active, yet always humble. His greatest service is in this manner of being.

With the Mahatma as a model, instead of money, pride, prestige, and power as a spur, the citizens of a democracy could begin to smooth out the conflicts, frictions, and injustices that limit the freedom and hamper the growth of individuals.

Beyond a certain variable point, money does not add to contentment. Indeed, the pursuit of money may cause unhappiness. The rich are quite as likely to feel insecure as the poor. The amassing of wealth for pleasure, power, and pride is a disease of the individual which spills over into a disease of society as a whole. If human beings could see this clearly (and they would if they asked themselves what it is all about and answered that question honestly), they might acquire a different sense of values. Today, for most people, money is the most valuable thing; it is the standard and measuring rod: "I feel like a million dollars."

The crazy emphasis on money as the ultimate value ruins individuality. Modern individualism rests precariously on what a person has, not on what he is. The two are not always the same.

"Rugged" individualists wasted the oil wealth of Pennsylvania. They wasted, and are still wasting, the timber of western United States. They enriched themselves and impoverished the community. Capitalistic individualism rewards the able, the well-trained, and the industrious; but it also awards the spoils to the strong, the shrewd, and the unscrupulous.

Gandhi's individualism grows out of his faith in nonviolence. With nothing but a sense of justice and his own determination, he defies the evil in power. When Gandhi defies money power he is anticapitalist. When he defies state power he is a democrat.

Gandhi is the antidote to Stalin because the Mahatma is the symbol of the individual against the strong government. Gandhi stood against the might of the British Empire—and won. He did it without money, without violence, and even without much organization. He did it with an idea and through the power that comes from honest means and honest words. Some will say it cannot work outside India. Who has tried?

Our society prides itself on its individualism, and almost every person believes that the road to wealth and fame is open to him. Yet the individual usually regards himself as socially insignificant and ineffective. Pose a problem of science or production or distribution to him and he attacks it with vigor and confidence. Pose the problem of poverty or politics or world peace to him and he says, "Nothing can be done about it." Our individualism is depriving the individual of almost all his capacities except those required to get money and power. Gandhi believes in the ability of individuals, either singly or through their organizations, to influence the course of major events.

Millions were ready to give their lives in the Second World War. Millions of civilians gave blood, work, money, time, and nerves to win that war. People are ready to die or live worse in order to win a war. They refuse to live better in order to prevent a war. Gandhiism asks people to live better. It does not ask them to live as saints in diapers. It asks them to be less selfish, less greedy, less money-mad, less self-centered; it asks them to be more kind, more honest, more friendly, more brotherly to those who are different, more public-spirited. No, some reply, that is too vague. It is vague until you meet the first person after getting up in the morning.

The teacher, student, official, factory owner, landlord, office manager, artist, editor, trolley conductor, policeman, shopkeeper, customer, worker can, by willing it, make a contribution practically every minute to his own and other people's happiness. Those with wealth and power can, within their present economic framework or by modifying it, improve living conditions.

Many persons behave much better toward their fellow-men than the law or their business or other relations require; they do so out of the goodness of their character. Everybody can behave better than he does. If we began to seek and use every opportunity for the improvement of self and society, the present mood of defeatism would vanish and people would not be saying, "I can do nothing about it. It's not up to me."

Gandhi's individualism rests on faith in man. "Do or die" is his favorite slogan. And since he does not want to die, his motto is "Do." The people who say they can do nothing about it are usually those who have not tried. All around us are social sores that need tending, politics that need purifying, injustices that need removing, economic changes that need urging.

At seventy-eight, against a million odds, Gandhi went into a blood-drenched area poisoned by hate and passion to deal with the difficult problem of Hindu-Moslem enmity. He moved some offenders to repent; others, among them murderers, surrendered to him or to the police; others gave money in expiation. He did not solve the problem, but the least he could do was to do the most he could.

Given a shelf of freedom on which to stand, and using the crowbar of individual power, Gandhi undertakes to move the earth. Few can be Gandhis, but one touch of Gandhi in each of us would add up to enough moral strength to defeat all the Stalins in Moscow and all the 50 per cent Stalins and Hitlers, and the 10 per cent and 2 per cent Stalins and Hitlers who dwell in the democracies and detract from the purity of democracy.

Defeating Stalin with Gandhi is the way to personal freedom and personal decency, and therefore to democracy, and therefore to peace.

Turn the searchlight inward.

Index